'It is one of the peculiar sentimentalities of the historian, this perpetual desire to trace places and origins by the shallow facts of romance.'
— **Lawrence Durrell**, *Prospero's Cell*

BY THE SAME AUTHOR

Travel

Romania Revisited

Fortresses of Faith

Revelations of Byzantium: the painted churches of Moldavia

Winds of Sorrow: Travels in and around Transylvania

Moons and Aurochs: A Romanian journey

Romanian Furrow by Donald Hall [Introduction]

History

The Discontented: Love, War and Betrayal in 17th century Hungary

Through Hitler's back door: SOE in Romania, Bulgaria, Hungary and Slovakia

A Spur called Courage: SOE in Italy

Sons of Odysseus: SOE in Greece

Tigers burning bright: SOE in the Far East

War of Shadows by Billy Moss [Afterword]

Terror by Night: The Official History of Raiding Forces Aegean [Introduction]

THE Vagabond AND THE Princess

PADDY LEIGH FERMOR *in* Romania

NINE ELMS BOOKS

The publisher and author wish to thank The Rațiu Family Charitable Foundation who have generously supported this publication.

The Vagabond and the Princess
Published in 2018 by Nine Elms Books Ltd

Unit 6B
Clapham North Arts Centre
26–32 Voltaire Road
London SW4 6DH

Email: inquiries@bene-factum.co.uk

www.bene-factum.co.uk

ISBN: 978-1-910533-35-2
e-book 978-1-910533-36-9 Epub

The photographs used are from the author's collection, the Cantacuzino family archive, the Stârcea-Mocsonyi archive, the V.A. Urechia Library [Galați] and from open licences in the public domain.

Cover, design and typesetting by Alex Thorton [www.alex22362.com]
Maps designed and drawn by Katyuli Lloyd [www.Katyuli.com]

Printed in the UK.

In memory of Șerban Cantacuzino [1928–2018],
a Prince of Kindliness

PREFACE

Romania was but one of many countries that Paddy Leigh Fermor traversed in his epic journey on foot from London to Istanbul in the 1930s. Yet it came to occupy centre stage in the three volumes of his entrancing account of his youthful peregrinations sequentially published some fifty years later. With each step across the complex tapestry of European national identities and cultural legacies, he had grown more confident and self-assured as he embraced the particular histories and absorbed the wisdom of hospitable mentors. Hungary was in many respects the first brush he had with the unfamiliar and once he had crossed the border into Romania, he discovered a romantic remote world where, free of inhibitions and conformity, he found his true self. He was by no means the first Englishman to become enamored with this alluring country on the edge of Europe.

Pre-war Romania attracted a coterie of English travel writers who have left us a variety of evocative accounts of their journeys, each configured by their particular motivation. Some were enthralled by the story of Queen Marie, the grand-daughter of Queen Victoria and wife of King Ferdinand of Romania. A beguiling and skillful publicist, 'Regina Maria' rarely turned down the opportunity to give an interview to her fellow countrymen. Dudley Heathcote [*My Wanderings in the Balkans, 1924*], Emile Hoppe [*In Gypsy Camp and Royal Palace, 1924*], Derek Patmore [*Invitation to Romania, 1939*] and Beverley Nichols [*No Place like Home, 1936*] all fell under her spell, usually over tea at Bran Castle.

Others like Donald Hall, fêted for his 1932 travelogue *Enchanted Sand: A New-Mexican Pilgrimage*, were drawn by the way of life of the Romanian peasants whose culture seemed impervious to the onward march of progress. In *Romanian Furrow* [1933] he donned peasant costume and went to live in a village on the southern slopes of the Carpathians. The writer and musicologist Philip Thornton ventured far and wide in search of local folk culture – *Dead Puppets Dance* [1937] and *Ikons and Oxen* [1939] – and his reports enthralled BBC audiences as he transported them from their armchairs in Croydon to the acrobatic dancing of the Căluşari and to the 'second' funeral of an old man near Craiova[1]. Henry Baerlein or 'H.B.', an extraordinary prolific travel writer, titillated his readers in *And then to Transylvania* [1931], *Enchanted Woods* [1932] and *Bessarabia and Beyond*

---

[1] He had died between Christmas and Epiphany, 'an unclean period' and was exhumed five years later on his Saint's Day for a second burial.

[1935] with stories of salacious encounters with Minerva, a shepherd-ess who seduced him in a hollow in the hills above Sibiu, and with the Cossack Grunia, 'a girl whose eyes were like buds of blue amber on dark velvet', who lured him into a wood like an amorous Dryad.

Gypsies with their itinerant way of life, dubbed by Liszt 'the outlaws of the human race', had long fascinated English authors such as George Borrow [*Lavengro* 1851], a trend not lost on the Romanian writer Konrad Bercovici in *Love and the Gypsy* [1923] which *The Glasgow Herald* lyrically wrote 'led [us] out to wolf-ridden forests, broad streams, and murmuring fields, to the company of Tartar and Gypsy Chiefs, and their dark-haired, tanned-skinned mistresses'. In *Singing Winds* [1926] and *The Story of the Gypsies* [1928], Bercovici extolls that 'there is more joy and more happi-ness, there is more poetry and deep emotion in a Gypsy camp of three ragged tents than in the largest city in our civilized world'. Walter Starkie, an eccentric and irascible Irish professor, told tales in *Raggle Taggle: ad-ventures with a fiddle in Hungary and Romania* [1933] of mad dogs, dodgy alcohol and ladies, mesmerized by the sound of his fiddle, undressing for him in hotel rooms.

Another traveller who was much taken by 'these thieves and liars with the look of ascetics who have fallen from grace' was Sacheverell Sitwell, who had met Paddy at a lunch with Princess Anne-Marie Callimachi and the sculptor and photographer Costa Achillopoulos in England in1936[2]. Shortly after, he set off to discover Romania, reputedly funded by King Carol II's government. Either by car or plane, he criss-crossed the country to piece together its history and culture. The end result, *Roumanian Jour-ney* [1938], is a flamboyant travelogue sprinkled with the adjective 'pictur-esque' and underpinned by Sitwell's authoritative voice as an art historian. Coming from his point of view that 'English literature is nearly silent where that country [Romania] is concerned', Sitwell's book represented a popular landmark in opening up the convoluted history and cultural secrets of the Romanian lands to English readers.

It is against this exotic backcloth of romantic novels, colourful reportage and histories of the 1930s, including R.W. Seton-Watson's heavyweight *History of the Roumanians* [1934], that Paddy's memories of his encounters in Romania made their belated appearance in 1986. By then, Romania had become a dark faraway country in the grip of Nicolae Ceaușescu, a Com-munist politician turned tyrannical fantasist who controlled his subjects through the machinery of his secret police, the ubiquitous and omniscient Securitate. If Paddy's account of his journey lacked the immediacy of his

---

[2] PLF introduction to Sitwell's *Roumanian Journey*, 7 March 1991.

pre-war peers, it gained in its intensity of conjuring up a long gone era. By happy accident, when Ceauşescu was toppled in 1989 and Romania slowly returned to her rightful place in a free Europe, *Between the Woods and the Water* proved the perfect inspiration for a new generation of travellers who set off to explore the former Iron Curtain countries.

Paddy's sojourns in Romania fall into two distinct and very different silos. The first, full to the brim with grains of truth ripened by the romance of youthful months of travel as a secular gyrovague and then refined by years of literary alchemy into a delicious blend of fact and fiction, is recorded in *Between the Woods and the Water* and *The Broken Road*. The second, five times as voluminous in terms of time, is only hinted at in *The Broken Road*. 'What happened was this. During the five years between the end of this journey and the outbreak of war, I returned several times to the countries we have so far crossed…Greece and Rumania were the two I visited, and lived in, most often. In Rumania I made two sojourns of about a year each…settled in the dales of High Moldavia. I travelled all over the country to the Delta, Bukovina, back to Transylvania, the Dobrudja, Bessarabia and to Bucharest many times'. This silo is almost empty save for a few carefully discarded flecks of memories of pre-war Moldavia which are encapsulated in a single article for *The Daily Telegraph* [later a chapter in *Words of Mercury*]. The same distillation process had been applied but the result this time is a pale, very private brew of guarded omissions and protective half-truths.

These contrasting depositories of times past are bridged by a wistfulness that like a prevailing wind permeates each crevice and cranny of Paddy's memory. From the early carefree days spent with the dispossessed Hungarian nobility in the lingering aftermath of the First World War and then with his muse and lover Princess Balaşa Cantacuzino as the belligerents of a second European war gathered on Romania's borders, Paddy sensed irreversible change, each moment tinged with a sense of imminent predestined loss. When he returned in the 1960s and 1980s, he was overwhelmed by the plight of his friends be it the confiscation of their property or the state sponsored theft of their liberty, dignity and potential. In this respect, Romania was unique in his *lebenssinn* and remained close to his heart throughout his long life.

A NOTE ON PADDY'S USAGE OF
PLACE NAMES AND TITLES

Cities, towns and villages in the former Hungarian lands in Romania are credited on many maps with both Romanian and Hungarian place names and, in the context of the Siebenbürgen in Transylvania, a German name as well. Paddy preferred to refer to them by their old non-Romanian names which is confusing for today's traveller. So I have used Romanian place names throughout, adding either the Hungarian and/or German name after the first reference to the place name.

Likewise, he uses the Hungarian word '*kastély*' to describe many of the houses he stayed in. It is akin to the French classification '*château*' in terms of the wide spectrum of size it encompasses. Its Romanian equivalent is '*castel*' which also includes large fortified quasi-military structures or '*var*' in Hungarian. Manor houses in Romania are known as *conacs* or, in Transylvania, sometimes as *curias* and the grandiose mansions of the 19th century '*riches, nouveaux et anciennes*' as a *palatul*.

Paddy styles several of his Hungarian hosts as 'von' which is incorrect for surnames with *praedicatum* are indicated in the Hungarian lands with the Latin 'de' (the language of Hungarian government administration and the judicial system was Latin until 1848) with a geographical place name of landed property or place of origin donated and issued by the monarch[1] e.g. Kintzig de Nyek, Klobusiczky de Klobusicz et Zétény. When a surname is used with 'von', it indicates a non-Magyar Austrian or German noble family established in Hungary with *indigenatus* (legal recognition of foreign nobility); in the case of French and Italian nobility, the 'de' simply continued.

However, when the Hungarian nobility travelled in Germany, Austria, or even France or Italy, they used 'von' most of the time e.g. von Zselénszky, which, although incorrect, reflected their pre-1918 Austrian orientation when German was invariably their second language. And, of course, all communications to the Emperor – *Seine kaiserliche und königliche Apostolische Majestät* – were signed off, using the German version.

In Hungarian, Christian names follow surnames, a convention which Paddy did not use, presumably to avoid confusion.

---

[1] Tötösy de Zepetnek, Steven. *nobilitashungariae: List of Historical Surnames of the Hungarian Nobility / A magyar történelmi nemesség családneveinek listája.* West Lafayette: Purdue University Press, 2010, http://docs.lib.purdue.edu/clcweblibrary/nobilitashungariae.

The Mocsonyi family, whom Paddy met on several occasions, pose a by no means atypical problem in terms of their nomenclature. As members of the Hungarian nobility, their title was Count Mocsonyi de Foen, yet post-1918 as prominent members of the Romanian political establishment, they were known as Mocioni. Their Christian names likewise chopped and changed according to the prevailing language. To avoid confusion and, with the kind permission of their heirs, I refer to them throughout by their Hungarian surname.

Finally, a word on the spelling of Cantacuzino. In Romanian, it is spelt Cantacuzino but in French 'Cantacuzène', in German 'Cantacuzen', in Russian 'Кантакузин' and in Greek Καντακουζηνός.

PART 1
1934

'The Castle of Vajhunyad[1] ...a building so fantastic and theatrical that, at first glance, it looked totally unreal'.

~ *Between the Woods and the Water*

The term 'gyrovague', like its ascetic practice, is a hybrid stemming from the Master's [St. Benedict] pairing of the Greek noun γυρο ['circle'] and the Latin verb *vagor* ['to roam about, wander, stroll']. This aberrant and unclean form of asceticism...hinges on its practitioners' uncanny talent for 'roaming in a circle'.

Lynda L. Coon: *Dark Age Bodies – gender and monastic practice in the early Medieval West*

---

[1] Should be spelt Vajdahunyad

ROMANIA IN 1934

The văcăreșteni, the founders of the Legion of the Archangel Michael
[Corneliu Codreanu sitting centre].

On 27 April 1934, a young Englishman crossed from Hungary into Romania at the sleepy border town of Curtici/Kürtös. His name was Paddy Leigh Fermor and his intention was to complete his walk from London to Istanbul which he has started some four months earlier. Passed from one well-connected grand family to another in Germany and Hungary, the youthful traveller's address book overflowed with introductions to members of the Hungarian nobility dotted around Crişana, the Banat and Transylvania. Fifty-two years later, the story of these early travels through Romania was published in his book, *Between the Woods and the Water.*

For the 19-year-old ingénue Paddy, what was this mysterious country called 'Roumania'? By his own admission, he had no interest in the politics of the day and he relied on his Hungarian hosts for historical context. With their national pride bloodied and bruised after a disastrous war, their nationality usurped and their properties eviscerated by alien land reforms, it is hardly surprising that much was left unsaid about Romania in their conversations with the young Englishman. A mere sixteen years had passed since the dismantlement of Austro-Hungary and most Hungarians were still in a state of shock, made worse by the eventual realization that the terms of the Treaty of Trianon would never be revised.

Romanian history has been dictated by the position she has occupied on the crossroads of imperial ambition – Roman, Bulgarian, Ottoman, Austrian and Russian. Thus for most of the last two thousand years, she has found herself often in the wrong place at the wrong time. That was her fate, not her fault. The fact is that through the adroit efforts of her rulers and through the perseverance and resilience of her people, Romania has survived and often prospered. And she has had her share of good fortune when the Habsburg Emperor drove the Turks out of Transylvania and the Banat in the late seventeenth century and much reduced the remit of the Ottomans; more good fortune when, as a result of the post-Crimean Treaty of Paris, the United Romanian Principalities of Wallachia and Moldavia emerged in 1859; and further good fortune when, as an outcome of the First World War, Transylvania was ceded by Austro-Hungary to Romania despite the humiliating peace treaty she had entered into with Germany in 1917.

In the spring of 1934, Romania was coming out of a series of upheavals, the latest being the Great Depression which had been exacerbated by two years of drought. From afar, there was more than a tint of Ruritania about it as foreign governments watched in askance the antics of the wayward Crown Prince Carol since 1918. Embroiled in a series of scandals, he had finally married Princess Helen of Greece who had dutifully produced an heir to the throne. It did not take long for Carol to stray when he met a 26-year-old socialite, Elena Lupescu. Within weeks she became his mistress and while on a tour of Europe with her, he renounced his right as heir to the throne. Thus, on the death of his father King Ferdinand in July 1927, it was Carol's son, the young Prince Michael, who was formally proclaimed King by the Romanian Parliament and a regency established under his uncle, Prince Nicholas. This incensed Carol and from then on he plotted his comeback. His first attempt failed and resulted in his expulsion from Britain, his haunt at the time. Finally, in 1930 when Juliu Maniu, the new Prime Minister, secretly agreed to his return as King in exchange for promises of good behaviour, he took off from Munich in a biplane and after a dramatic and dangerous flight landed at Bucharest's Baneasa airport late on the night of 7 June.

Reneging on the promises he had made to Maniu, King Carol promptly installed Elena Lupescu in Modrogan Park and as the politician Constantin Argetoianu pithily put it, 'if a person approved their relationship, he was the King's friend; if he opposed it, he was the King's enemy'. Surrounded by a *camarilla* of powerful courtiers including the wealthy industrialists Nicolae Malaxa and Max Aushnitt and the banker Aristide Blank, Carol presided over an ineffective testy government which lurched from crisis to crisis. On 29 December 1933, Prime Minister Ion Duca was assassinated by the Iron Guard, gunned down in a snow storm at Sinaia railway station while he waited for the last train to Bucharest.

Founded in 1927 as the Legion of the Archangel Michael, the Iron Guard was a homegrown Romanian fascist movement whose roots originated in the chaotic economic conditions of northeast Moldavia after the First World War. Intensely nationalistic and anti-Semitic, its charismatic handsome leader Corneliu Codreanu adopted the typical paraphernalia of fascism, in his case green shirts to symbolize the renewal of the Romanian spring, and in common with Hitler and Mussolini, the Roman salute and a paramilitary structure. However, unlike the other European fascist movements, the Legion embraced religion and celebrated the mysticism of the Orthodox rite. Codreanu envisaged a new order based on the political purity of the Romanian peasants; Romania did not need new political programmes but men of virtue to replace the decadent ruling class. He would enter a village on horseback, often dressed in white with a cross in his hand, and bless the peasants who greeted him with candles and flowers, some even prostrating themselves on the ground in front of him. By 1934, the Legion had become a force to be reckoned which allowed Codreanu to float the idea of a Legionary state with the King as its head. The only obstacle to this proposal was Lupescu and her camarilla which soon became the target of the Legion's hatred. Already deeply unpopular, the 'Down with the camarilla' campaign orchestrated by the Legion galvanized Lupsecu and her cronies to try and poison Codreanu in the summer of 1934. It failed and from then there was no chance of reconciliation.

Romania was not alone in contending with the instability in the Balkans which followed the First World War and the demise of Austro-Hungary. The Internal Macedonian Revolutionary Movement [IMRO] terrorized both Bulgaria, Greece and Yugoslavia in its attempt to create an independent Macedonian state; its victims included Alexander Stamboliski, the Bulgarian Prime Minister, whose head was delivered in a biscuit tin to Parliament in 1923, and King Alexander I of Yugoslavia, together with the French Foreign Minister, on a Yugoslavian state visit to France in 1934. The Croatian separatist organization, Ustashe, entered the political fray in the early 1930s with a similar murderous programme of terror and assassinations.

This then was the Romania that Paddy ventured into, Malcolm Arnold's scholar gypsy 'of pregnant parts and quick inventive brain, who, tired of knocking at preferment's door, one summer morn forsook his friends, and went to learn the gypsy lore'. In Paddy's case his preferment was the curious and nostalgic milieu of the *Mitteleuropaische* nobility. At the time, he was seemingly oblivious to the historical struggle of the Romanians for recognition as a people ['*natio*'] in a world defined by the Enlightenment and the ascendancy of an anti-imperialist America as the beacon of democracy.

Closeted with Hungarians, the young Paddy was in effect quarantined from the Romanians around him, be they intellectuals, politicians, businessmen, landowners or agricultural labourers, the latter usually referred to as 'peasants' but not in a detrimental fashion. So, in order to set the scene in the context of the Greater Romania of 1920, one needs to travel back in time.

The Hungarian lands in Romania – a Romanian perspective.

Ten miles north of the bustling city of Arad, the 16th century town of Curtici lies in the old military frontier region that once delineated the front lines of the Habsburg and Ottoman empires for nearly two hundred years. Paddy could not have chosen a more symbolic crossing point, for this part of Romania, Crișana, is defined by the course of the River Mureș/Maros that runs from East to West and the Apuseni Mountains to the East. To the North and East lies Transylvania, to the South an area known as the Banat and Crișana itself, once known as the Partium or Részek in Hungarian, marches with Western Hungary.[1]

Arad straddles the River Mureș, the great glittering thread of Transylvanian commerce and trade for two thousand years. It was down this river that salt was exported to the rest of Europe, raising in modern terms millions of pounds for the Hungarian and then Habsburg treasuries. Originally mined on the surface by the Romans – *salina* is Latin – the industry developed into massive subterranean mines, the largest at Turda and Praid, others at Vizakna, Kolozs, Désakna and Maros Ujvár. This great river joins the Tisza sixty miles to the West at Szeged, from where they both flow into the Danube at Slankamen. The names of rivers reveal their antiquity – Mureș, Maros in Hungarian, Μαϱιξ in Greek, probably originated as a Thracian word for 'swampy' or 'boggy'.

---

[1] The Partium, more or less, belonged to the Principality of Transylvania from 1542 to 1690. After the expulsion of the Ottomans, it was ruled directly from Vienna until the 1867 Ausgleich when it was incorporated into Austro-Hungary. In 1920, 60% was ceded to Romania.

The modern history of Transylvania began in 1000 AD when the Kingdom of Hungary was founded. The word 'Transylvania' is Latin for 'the land beyond the forests'. However, the earliest references to this area, found in 12th century documents of the Royal Hungarian Chancellery, use a different word, 'Ultrasylvania', implying that the land did not yet belong in its entirety to the Hungarian King. It would only be his if he took steps to secure it.

Once the Hungarians had completed their conquest of Transylvania, a Hungarian *comes* or count based in Alba Julia was appointed as ruler. Apart from the obvious attractions of additional land and a defensible border of mountain ridges, there were other prizes that came with the territory – salt, gold and silver, three commodities of enormous value in the Middle Ages. Little wonder that the sale of salt, easily transported down the rivers in blocks hewn from vast underground caverns, later became a royal prerogative of the Habsburg Emperors.

Transylvania quickly became key to the defence of the Hungarian Kingdom in the East and, as attacks by marauding Steppe warriors increased, it was placed under the jurisdiction of a special royal officer, the *vajda*, who by 1263 had the right to appoint *comes* for the seven Transylvanian counties. Transylvania therefore became almost a kingdom within a kingdom. It is in the twelfth and thirteenth centuries that the first traces of the Romanians in Transylvania are found in historic documents. They are mentioned as nomadic, pastoral people who roamed about the Balkans and in the summer months sought pasture for their cattle in the Transylvanian mountains.

Then, in 1396, Sigismund of Luxembourg, King of Hungary for fifty years and Emperor of the Holy Roman Empire for fifteen, at the head of an immense Crusading army of 100,000 men, suffered a resounding and bloody defeat at the hands of the Ottomans at Nicopolis. His crusade came to an abrupt end. Indeed, it was to be the last crusade and the beginning of Ottoman ascendancy in Eastern and Central Europe.

Hungary experienced a similar setback in 1526 when young King Lajos II died after being thrown from his horse after being defeated by Sultan Suleiman the Magnificent at Mohács, a disaster that led to the eventual relinquishment of much of Hungary to the avaricious Ottoman Empire. The throne passed to his bother-in-law, Ferdinand Habsburg, Archduke of Austria and Holy Roman Emperor, an equally inauspicious event as it turned out for subsequent German Emperors had little time for Hungarian national aspirations.

For a short period, when the Ottomans were masters of Buda [modern day Budapest] and the eastern Hungarian lands, Transylvania became an autonomous principality, balanced on the precarious tightrope between Vienna and Istanbul. Its princes depended on the permissions of the Sultan, the mood of the Emperor and the goodwill of their own Diet. Beneath the surface simmered Hungarian anger against Turks and Germans alike. It was nevertheless a Golden Age in that, under the guidance of the remarkable Prince Gábor Bethlen, the Principality won recognition in the courts of Europe while at the same pioneering some remarkable legislation in the fields of education and religious tolerance.

When the Habsburg Emperors finally expelled the Turks from Hungary, the status of Transylvania as an independent principality also came to an end; the Diploma Leopoldinum promulgated in December 1691 effectively transformed it into an Austrian province. However, the two principalities of Moldavia and Wallachia on Transylvania's eastern and southern borders remained under Turkish suzerainty and their Greek Phanariot[2] princes, appointed by the Sultans as 'commission men', taxed the hapless populace to such a degree of impoverishment that many emigrated West and North into Transylvania.

By 1761 according to an Imperial census, Transylvanian Romanians totalled 787,000, thereby forming a majority of the Transylvanian population. Yet still they were excluded from participating in official political or religious life; under the Hungarian feudal system, they formed no *recepta natio* and thus were allowed no political organization and likewise their religion, the Orthodox church, did not rank as a *recepta religio*.

The agent for change came in the unlikely form of the Emperor Joseph. On the death of his mother and co-Regent, the Empress Maria Theresa, he turned his reforming zeal to Transylvania; he had been appalled at its backwardness on his visit there in 1773 when he received nearly 19,000 petitions. In 1781, he introduced *Concivilität* – citizenship for all – and the abolition of torture to extract confessions.

On his second Transylvanian visit in 1783, Joseph issued a decree of emancipation for the serfs, which the Hungarian nobility refused to implement thereby triggering a bloody peasants' revolt. Three Romanian leaders – Horia, Closça and Crişau – stepped forward to voice the collective concerns of the peasants. Events spun out of control as thousands of primitively armed peasants went on the rampage in the Abrud and along the Mureş valley. By the time this outburst of anger had been brought under control, 230 castles and manor houses lay ruined or looted and over 100 members of the nobility murdered. Joseph now had to close Pandora's

---

[2] Phanar was and still is the Greek quarter in Istanbul half way along the Golden Horn.

box. Before an invited audience of 2,500 peasants, Horia and Closça were broken on the wheel, then disembowelled alive; their limbs were stuck on pikes and distributed to the crowd as keepsakes.

The forces of reaction, never far below the surface in the Habsburg Empire, found a more malleable leader in Joseph's successor, Leopold II. Whilst remaining sympathetic to the plight of the Transylvanian Romanians, he put the issue of Transylvania on ice for the alarming and thoroughly unsavoury revolution in France now dictated his priorities: no more political experiments, only the upholding of law and order. When the leaders of the Romanians appealed to the Emperor in 1791 in a memorandum, the '*Supplex Libellus Valachorum*', asking for the recognition of the Romanians as a *natio* and for equal rights and privileges with the other *nati*, it was ignored.

For the next thirty years, the issue of Transylvania gathered dust on the Chancellery shelves in Vienna until 1835, when the Transylvanian diet was revived as a form of self-governance in the wake of a similar arrangements granted by Vienna to the Hungarians in the 1820s. The three *nati* – Hungarians, Székelys and Saxons – settled down to collaborative government, which continued to exclude the Romanian majority. When in 1840, Hungarian superseded Latin as the official language of the Hungarian Government and Parliament, the Transylvania Saxon Pastor, Stephan Roth, pointed out that when making a journey or visiting a market, 'before one tries to see whether one speaks German or the other Magyar, the conversation begins in the Wallach language' and published a book in 1842, *Der Sprachkampf in Siebenbürgen,* which argued in favour of Romanian as Transylvania's primary language. For his plain speaking, the Hungarians later executed him by firing squad on the battlements of Cluj in 1849.

With the introduction of Hungarian as a common language came a parallel demand by the demagogue Lajos Kossuth, the arch proponent of Magyarisation, for the re-union of Transylvania with Hungary. As soon as the news of the February 1848 Revolution in Paris reached Bratislava, the Hungarian parliament decamped and returned to its ancient seat in Budapest and on 1 April union with Transylvania was proclaimed to the delight of the Hungarian minority and to the horror of the Saxons and Romanians. When 6,000 Romanians gathered at Blaj in May 1848 to hear their leader, Bishop Raţiu, proclaim "now let us be free men", it triggered a wave of nationalist fervour. Three weeks later, the crowd had swelled to 40,000 and was demanding proportional representation for the Transylvanian Romanian *natio*.

By the spring of 1848, the tide of revolution had been stemmed; the Habsburgs had crushed the uprising in Milan (Savoy) and turned their attention to the far greater problem of how to suppress the impudent Hungarian independence movement. After quickly putting their own house in order by suppressing revolts in Prague and Vienna and by changing Emperors, the *Hofburg* gave the task of bringing Hungary back into the fold to two Imperial Generals, Alfred Windischgrätz and his brother-in-law, Felix von Schwarzenberg. Both men had no time for the 'nationalities'.

Transylvania became a battleground. Kossuth, the President of newly independent Hungary, appointed the diminutive but dynamic Polish General, József Bem, to defend Transylvania against the Imperial troops. He then declared himself Governor of Hungary in April 1849, thus provoking the Habsburgs to invite the Russians to assist them. Two hundred thousand of the Tsar's men poured into Hungary from the North. Kossuth's 'hussars', brilliantly led by Bem, staged a courageous and desperate defence but, outnumbered two to one, were defeated by the Russians at Sighişoara/Segesvár in July. By October, Hungary itself had been reduced once more to the status of an Austrian province, with Transylvania ironically placed 'under the protection' of Vienna. The irrepressible Bem fled to Istanbul where he converted to Islam and under the name of Amurat Murad Pasha ended his days as governor of Aleppo.

But to the delight of Vienna, order had been restored in Transylvania – the Diet was stood down, a governor appointed and a visit arranged for yet another Habsburg Emperor to promote *Felix Austria*. For now, the Saxons were the only happy *natio* in Transylvania for German had been re-introduced as the official language. Thus, it was no coincidence that when the Transylvanian diet was finally reconvened, it was in Sibiu, the twelfth century capital of the Saxon settlers.

Suddenly there was a glimmer of hope for a lasting accord; the three languages – Hungarian, German and Romanian – were given equality, the Orthodox Church was put on an equal footing with its peers and the question of Romanian political representation addressed. But, with the Prussian victory over the Austrians at Sadová in 1866, the light soon faded. Ignominiously forced to hand Venice over to a 'defeated' Italy, Franz-Joseph had little option other than to settle with the Hungarians; if he didn't, the chances were that he would lose Hungary and the Empire would become an Austrian only affair. The result was a compromise – the *Augsleich* of 1867 – when the Hungarians were given internal self-government and Austria-Hungary became a dual monarchy under the Habsburgs.

In April 1884, a new Romanian language newspaper *Tribuna* appeared

on the streets of Sibiu. It pulled no punches – 'we are not going to in-
vestigate whether the Romanians dissatisfaction is well-founded; there is
no denying it exists as an elementary calamity'. Within four years, a libel
suit had been brought by the authorities against the paper and its editor,
Slavici, imprisoned in the Danubian town of Vác. But Romanian nationalism was far from silenced; the war of words continued with a lively student
pamphlet campaign and Ioan Rațiu, a leading nationalist, was for the first
time positive about progress – 'Our grievances have been publicized all
over Europe; it is not our fault that European public opinion has finally
realised that something is rotten in this country.'

The frustrations of the Transylvanian Romanians were once again ex-
pressed in a Memorandum to the Emperor – 'after 25 years of constitu-
tional rule, the antagonisms are deeper than ever….(Romanians) can no
longer trust the Budapest parliament or the Hungarian government'. A
delegation of 237 Romanians, led by Rațiu, set off to Vienna in May 1892.
Their purpose was to bring charges against Hungary's king to the attention
of the Austrian Emperor; they were of course one and the same person.
The sealed envelope containing the memorandum was deposited at the
cabinet office from where it was forwarded to Budapest and then returned
by the Prime Minister's office to Rațiu's home address – unopened.

Romanian failure was unexpectedly reversed when Turda's Hungarian
community attacked Rațiu's house. This provoked an outcry and soon over
13,000 copies of the unread memorandum had been published in Sibiu
with nearly 2,000 sent abroad. State prosecutors soon brought charges
against the signatories as well as those who admitted responsibility for
preparing it and a trial opened in Cluj/Kolozsvár in May 1894. In the
great hall of the *Redout*, a splendid eighteenth century building usually
the setting of glamorous winter balls and bouts of decadent gambling, the
defendants planned to turn what was billed as a routine libel trial into a
major political confrontation.

Rațiu made an impassioned speech, reminding his prosecutors 'a people is not an issue for discussion, it is for assertion'. The Hungarians and
Romanian nations had been 'locked in litigious conflict for a hundred
years' and there was 'another, higher court, a more enlightened and less
prejudiced one, that will bring judgment: the jury of the cultured world,
which one day will judge and condemn you with greater severity than this
one can. If we are condemned in a spirit of impatience and by a racial
fanaticism that has no equal in Europe, it will prove to the world that the
Hungarians are a discordant element in the realm of civilization.' After
seventeen days, the trial ended. Four defendants were found not guilty and
acquitted; the remainder were found guilty and imprisoned.

Twenty years later, at the beginning of the First World War, Austro-Hungary committed herself to an alliance with Germany and Turkey. Sitting on the periphery of the conflict, Romania remained neutral until the summer of 1916 when she entered into the war on the side of the Allies, a decision which would ultimately result in the long-deferred emancipation of Transylvania's Romanian majority. In October 1918, the Romanian National Party met at Oradea and invoked the right of self-determination for the Romanians of Hungary, the same time that President Wilson recognised the Kingdom of Serbs, Croats and Slovenes [Yugoslavia] and the Czechoslovak National Council. The Habsburg empire had finally dissolved into its component parts – Galicia and Ruthenia seceded – causing Greater Hungary to disintegrate. The leaders of the Transylvanian Romanians convoked a National Assembly on 1 December in Blaj, without inviting the Hungarian and Saxon *nati* to attend. This assembly, cheered by thousands of peasants, declared for the union of Transylvania with Romania in the name of "all the Romanians of Transylvania, the Banat, and Hungary". The Hungarians, by now in total disarray, were powerless to resist.

No wonder Paddy's Hungarian hosts felt aggrieved and disinclined to socialize with their new Romanian overlords.

The Banat – the odd man out

By a quirk of a few hundred metres, the majority of Paddy's hosts lived south of the River Mureş, that is to say in the old Banat. Best known as the flash point of the 1989 revolution – over 1,000 civilians were killed here between 16 and 21 December – its capital Timişoara/Temesvár was put on the modern map by the Romans, who grasping its strategic importance as 'a turtle in the middle of a marsh', built a camp there on the old Dacian settlement of Zambara. That fort was to dictate the town's history. Possibly a Cuman settlement in the eleventh century, Andreas II of Hungary recognised it as *Castrum Temesiensis* in 1212 and soon it became Temesvár, the capital of the Banat, an area that encompasses the South-West corner of modern Romania. Almost a perfect square, its boundaries follow the River Mureş East from Szeged to Zam; South from Zam to Orsova; West along the Danube to Belgrade and then back North to Szeged.

A particularly gory episode was enacted in the city in the early sixteenth century. A Hungarian peasants' revolt over 70,000 strong led by György Doja arrived beneath the city walls in the summer of 1514 and laid it to siege. The timely arrival of the Prince of Transylvania's forces saved the day and over forty of the rebel leaders were captured. After fifteen days of unrelenting torture, only ten were left alive including Doja. Forced to sit on a red-hot iron throne, he was, in a word, barbequed. The nine other survivors were forced to eat his flesh before the remains of his body were quartered and sent to various cities for public display.

The Banat was the first area to be occupied by the Ottomans after the defeat and death of the Hungarian King Louis II at the Battle of Mohács in 1526. After a hard-fought siege, Timișoara surrendered in 1552 and the head of the Spanish mercenary captain in charge of its defence, Alfonso Perez, was scalped, stuffed and sent to the Sultan. Now an Ottoman province – Eyālet-i Tımışvār – Ottoman rule was harsh, especially the fiscal burden, so many peasants voted with their feet and, before long, vast rural swathes of the Banat were almost deserted. The city itself continued to prosper as a trading centre, as evidenced by the Turkish traveller Evlie Celebi who found over 400 shops there in 1660.

After over three hundred years of intermittent military confrontation, in September and October 1716 the Habsburg Imperial Army, commanded by the brilliant general, Prince Eugene of Savoy, finally succeeded in driving the Ottomans out and the province was ceded to the Habsburg Emperor Charles VI at the Treaty of Passarowitz in July 1718 after 164 years of Ottoman rule. The Banat of Temesvár, as it was now called, was considered a crown territory of the Holy Roman Empire and from 1718 to 1778 was administered from Vienna; from 1778 to 1848 it was incorporated into the political administration of Hungary.

The expulsion of the Turks in 1718 resulted in a resettlement program sponsored by the Habsburgs to bolster the meagre number of inhabitants left in the area, mainly Serbs. They offered Catholics of the South-western German states inducements such as free agricultural land, building plots, construction materials, livestock and exemption from taxes for several years. The colonization of the Banat was entrusted to one of Prince Eugene's generals, Claudius Florimund, Count of Mercy. He sent his agents to Baden, Würtemberg, Alsace, Lorraine, the Rhinelands, Westphalia, Bavaria and Swabia as well as other areas. Confronted by this *pot pourri* of new arrivals from various regions and speaking various dialects, the Hungarians decided to call them Swabians, and the name came to be applied to all the Germans who settled in the Danube valley

The colonization came to be known as *der Grosse Schwabenzuge* or The Great Swabian Trek. The majority of the migration took place in three phases which were named after their Habsburg sponsors: the 15,000-strong 'Karolinische Ansiedlung' from 1718–37; the 75,000 'Maria Theresianische Ansiedlung' from 1744–72; and the 60,000 'Josephinische Ansiedlung' from 1782–1787. A Swabian ditty succinctly classifies them as:

Die Erste hat den Tod,
Der Zweite hat die Not
Der Dritte erst hat Brot.

The first encounters death[3],
The second need,
Only the third has bread.

During these migrations, other nationalities also settled in the plains of the Banat, among them Serbs, Croatians, Bulgarians and Romanians, and to a lesser extent, Slovaks, Ruthenians, Czechs and a few French and Italians. By the end of eighteenth century, more than 1,000 German villages had been established in the Banat and by the end of the next century, there were more than two million Germans living in the Hungarian territories.

1848 brought demands for independence by both the Romanians and the Serbs of the Banat. Worried by the increasing stridency of the Serbian minority, the Hungarian nationalists at first showed some sympathy for this aspiration but soon the shutters came down and in 1849 direct rule was re-imposed by Vienna until the *augsleich* of 1867 when the Banat formally became part of Hungary.

When the revised final boundaries for Hungary were agreed at the Treaty of Trianon in June, 1920, the Banat was awarded to Romania. Yugoslavia gained land in Southern Hungary, including a strip of the Western Banat. The Swabian villagers whose families had lived there for almost 200 years now found themselves in two different countries, neither of which was Hungary.

So clearly Paddy had unknowingly crossed a historical crevasse when he ventured south of the great river.

The upheavals of 1918 – 1934

The upheavals previously referred to describe the Romania of 1934 that Paddy encountered as he crossed the border at Curtuci were primarily the result of land reform spurred on by political necessity and expediency.

In 1934 the impact on the Hungarians of the momentous events of 1918 were still raw. Determined to soak up the history and language of the region, Paddy's sole exposure to politics was through the medium of his Hungarian hosts to whom Bucharest appeared 'a faraway Babylon of dust and bribery and wickedness'. Nearly all of them were landowners whose

---

[3] From 1749 to 1771, over 9,651 were buried in the parish of the citadel in Timisoara alone. Considering that the population of the city in 1771 was about 10,000, an entire generation was wiped out by the plague, war and earthquakes.

lifestyle and livelihood had recently been diminished. Although he wrote in *Between the Woods and the Water* that 'there was hardly a trace of this distress [caused by land reform]...detectable to a stranger' for 'estates, much reduced, existed still', he later added in his introduction to the English translation of Miklós Bánffy's *They Were Counted* that 'the old Hungarian landowners felt stranded and ill-used by history; nobody likes having a new nationality forced on them, still less, losing estates by expropriation. This, of course, is what happened to the descendants of the old feudal landowners of Transylvania'. However, they were not alone.

Land reform in Romania – the former principalities of Wallachia and Moldavia – had been triggered by fear of a Communist revolution. Indeed a Peasants' Revolt in 1907 had had to be put down by force, resulting in the deaths of an estimated 11,000 people. In March 1917, with the Russian Revolution in full swing just across its eastern border, King Ferdinand set in motion a series of radical agrarian reforms to appease his largely peasant army which the Romanian government[4] implemented in 1921. While each of the ten regions had its own property law, reflecting its social and economic make-up, the overall objective was the transfer of land to the peasants through the breakup of estates. For Romanians in Wallachia and Moldavia, the limit for arable land was set at 600 acres; for those in the former Banat, Transylvania, Bessarabia and Bucovina, it was 200 acres. Forest holdings were more generously treated.

The reforms of 30 July 1921 that applied to Transylvania and the Banat followed the newly redrawn borders in accordance with the Treaty of Trianon. All in all, Hungary lost 66 per cent of her territory (compared to Germany's 13.5 per cent) and 3.4 million of her people were now outside of her borders. For the Hungarians, there was disbelief after Trianon. Their reaction was '*nem, nem, soha* – no, no, never' and it was the scion of one of the great Transylvanian families, Pál Teleki, who took on the role of Prime Minister to 'save Hungary from abominable dismemberment'. He failed and when Paddy met him in Budapest in 1934, Pál had left politics and reverted to his academic discipline of geography.

Transylvania had been ceded to Romania and the Banat split between Romania and Serbia. In these former 'foreign-owned' lands [including former Russian-owned Bessarabia], land reforms were executed by the bureaucrats in Bucharest with a nationalistic fervor unlike the more relaxed

---

[4] David Mitrany: *The Land and the Peasant in Romania – the War and Agrarian Reform 1917–1921.*

transition enjoyed by Romanians.[5] Furthermore the terms of compensation for former Hungarian owners were blatantly harsh: expropriation prices were fixed by the government as an average of prices from 1908-1913 which amounted to about 5 per cent of current prices including currency depreciation. Payment was in non-transferable government bonds bearing an interest rate of 5% and redeemable in 1971. The market value of these bonds was 30-40% of face value which meant that owners received a fraction of the real value of their properties. The terms for landowners in the Banat were markedly less severe, reflecting their closer links with Bucharest and Belgrade.

The great estates of the Hungarian nobility and the land holdings of Hungarian institutions such as churches and schools were thus dismantled throughout the former Hungarian lands. In pre-1914 Hungary which included Transylvania, 324 large landowners held over 20% of the arable land with an average holding of 41,000 acres – the Catholic Church itself accounted for over a million. However, it is important to differentiate between Hungarian and Transylvanian large landholdings: at the time of the 1867 *Ausgleich*, the majority of the Transylvanian nobility — some 3,500 — owned land ranging in area from 57 to 285 hectares, while a minority had estates of 285 to 2,850 hectares. In 1900, only one Transylvanian figured among Hungary's hundred biggest landowners, Count György Bánffy, who reportedly owned 14,644 hectares, much of it woodland. Contrast that to Prince Pál Esterházy who owned 135,000 hectares in Hungary proper[6].

For most of the medium size Transylvanian landowners, life since the 1850s had never been easy. Facing not only the familiar fluctuation of agricultural commodity prices[7] but also the increasing reluctance of banks to lend them money to maintain their outmoded lifestyles rather than for tangible agricultural improvements and modernization, they sold off parcels of land and encouraged their children to seek jobs in government service or the professions[8]. Estates could not be entailed and consequently were fragmented through Salic inheritance law.

---

[5] Romanian landowners i.e. the great estates in Wallachia and Moldavia were by no means exempt – large farm holdings in excess of 100 hectares declined from 8.1m to 1.9 m hectares by 1930.

[6] Leland Stowe: *Foreign Affairs* April 1947.

[7] Grain prices collapsed in 1895 and only recovered in 1905 when protectionist tariffs were introduced.

[8] According to the Transylvanian Economic Association, the number of Hungarian middle landowners decreased by 25 percent between 1900 and 1914.

So the *demise de grandeur* which Paddy encountered in 1934 was as much of a continuum rather than the shock of punitive land reform which merely exacerbated a downward economic trend of which the Liberal MP Count István Bethlen[9] had sounded the alarm in 1913: "The Hungarians of Transylvania are on the brink of economic and political ruin." The Great Depression also played its part for agricultural prices halved between 1928/29 and 1933/34.

When Paddy writes in his introduction to Miklós Bánffy's *Transylvanian Trilogy* that 'remnants of the old estates did still exist', there was a confluence of factors that accounted for their enormous reduction. He captures the mood perfectly for 'charm and douceur de vivre was still afloat among the faded décor and the still undiminished libraries, and, out of doors, everything conspired to delight. Islanded in the rustic Romanian multitude…and, with the phantoms of their lost ascendancy still about them, the prevailing atmosphere conjured up the tumbling demesnes of the Anglo-Irish in Waterford or Galway with their sadness and their magic'.

Tom Fort in *Against the Flow* admirably catches the essence of Paddy's first Romanian journey in *Between the Woods and the Water*. 'Although academic historians may frown on its lack of gritty social realism, Leigh Fermor's realisation of the sunlit curtain call of the Central European aristocracy has not lost its power to dazzle and beguile. It conjures up a world of great houses standing in magnificent parks with limitless estates extending beyond the soaring limes and spreading oaks…the seductiveness of this portrait – real or not – is intensified by our awareness that this whole world was about to crash. Within a few years the counts and countesses who had entertained the young Englishman would be scattered to the four winds'.

There was to be a sting in the tail of what the writer and broadcaster Philip Thornton referred to as 'the idiotic re-shuffle of land which hoped to stop any further fighting'.[10] After backing away from a confrontation with Russia after it had seized Bessarabia and Bucovina in late June 1940 [with the cognizance of Germany], Romania had to give half of Transylvania back to Hungary in compliance with the Second Vienna Award arbitrated by Germany and Italy. As if this was not galling enough, further national humiliation followed when Italy demanded the return of the Southern Dobrudja to Bulgaria, another Axis ally. With France, her only protector, now under German occupation, it was inevitable that Romania shuffled into the Axis tent to recover her eastern lands. The punitive Treaty of

---

[9] Later PM of Hungary from 1921–1931.

[10] *Ikons and Oxen*

Trianon and the ensuing dismemberment of Hungary had given Hitler all the bargaining chips he needed.

Paddy's Transylvania of '*grandes battues* where the guns were all Purdeys. Gossip, cigar smoke and Anglophilia floated in the air…hundreds of acres of forest were nightly lost at *chemin de fer*, at day-break lovers stole away from tousled four-posters through secret doors, and duels were fought, as they still were when I was there'[11] had long gone.

---

[11] Introduction to *Transylvanian Trilogy*

Solymossy kastély at Mocrea

Solymossy kastély at Mocrea 2017

Zselénszky house 2017

Kintzig kastély at Scanteia 1911

Hotel Domeniul Lupaş 2017

Interior of Kintzig kastély 1903 and 2017

Castelul Nopcsa at Zam [Xenia Csernovics]

Spitalul de Psihiatrie Zam 2017

Gróf Károlyi Gyula kastélya. Mácsa.

The Csernovics kastély at Macea, lost in a card game

Teleki kastély at Căpâlnaş

Spitalul de Psihiatrie Căpâlnaş 2017

Woodland gravestones of Count Jenő Teleki and his daughter Mady

Mausoleum (inset) and Mocsonyi kastély at Foeni

Mocsonyi kastély 2017

'István' Elemér Klobusiczky's videki Kastély at Gurasada

Mănăstirea Maria Radna, 1910 and 2017

Konopi kastély at Odvoş 1910

Odvoş 2017

The chapel at Odvoș and Kalman Konopi's memorial

Count Ferenc Hunyady's kastély at Săvârşin

Royal Castelul Săvârşin 2017

Mocsonyi kastély at Bulci 1920

Mocsonyi kastély at Bulci

Tomești; the glashutte works; Winkler house

Chapter Two

HUNGARIAN HOSTS AND HOSTESSES

'Not that I had seen the last of the Hungarians, thank Heavens: pre-arranged stopping-places already sprinkled the western marches of Transylvania'.

~ *Between the Woods and the Water*

There are seven gates or entrances to Transylvania, an upland region dramatically enclosed by mountains and high forests. Ineu/Jenőfalva sits astride the gate that opens into the *Țara Zarandului* or Zărand, an area to the north of the Mureş River famed for its gold and silver mines. Given its strategic position, Ineu and its castle has had a life full of vicissitudes, its ownership defined by the powerful currents of history that have swept through these borderlands between East and West. First it belonged to the Losonczy de Angyalos family for two hundred years until 1566 when a Turkish army occupied the town. Then it was the turn of the Transylvanian princes, the Báthorys, Bethlens and Rákóczis to own it until 1658 when the Turks once again took over. When the Ottomans were finally ejected from Transylvania in 1690, Ineu became a possession of the Austrian emperors. The castle was last renovated in 1870 in a Neo-Classical style, and functioned as an Austrian-Hungarian army barracks until 1901. Later it became an orphanage until abandoned in 1996. Today it forlornly waits for someone to buy it and give it a new lease of life.

Paddy's first host was 44-year-old Baron Tibor Solymossy de Loos et Egervar whose house lies just to the south of Ineu in the hamlet of Mocrea/Apatelek. Built in Neo-Classical style in 1834 by Baron Sándor Atzél de Borosjenő, the Solymossy de Loós et Egervár family had acquired it in 1879 from his nephew Peter Atzél, who had started up a timber company with the Viennese entrepreneur Johann Sepper before falling on hard times.

Paddy had previously met Baron Tibor in Budapest. A former military man, who had fought throughout the First World War[1], the Baron had extended an invitation to him to come and stay. The two men chanced upon one another at the end of market day in Ineu and soon were 'bowling off to the hills' where they turned through tall gates and alighted in front of a Palladian façade 'just as night was falling'. Awaiting them was Ria Bielek, the daughter of an impoverished Polish music publisher in Cracow, whose role was to act as hostess in a bachelor household. Paddy was soon transfixed by her – 'everyone loved her, and so did I'.

Spending the mornings between the library and an outdoor table, Paddy immersed himself in Central European history, occasionally distracted by exotic feathered visitors such as golden orioles, bee-eaters and hoopoes. When Tibor's sister[2] arrived with friends from Vienna, 'there was much festivity and dressing up and picnics', culminating in a midnight feast on the summit of 'the vine-clad hemispherical hill of Mokra (that) soared like a volcanic island against snowy heaps of cloud and a pale sky'.

One afternoon, Tibor drove Paddy into Arad to visit a 'tall, dark and very pretty girl called Ilona', who lived in a discrete and leafy street leading down to the Mureş. As consolation for his guest, Ilona had arranged for her friend Izabella to entertain Paddy. The end result was a sketch in his journal that somehow survived the wear and tear of his travels. Dated 'Arad 16 May 1934', it marked the end of his three week stay with Tibor and the enchanting Ria.

---

[1] His younger brother Gabor had been killed on the Eastern front less than two weeks into the war.

[2] He had two sisters – Márta who was married to Janos Pallavicini and lived in Zemplén in northern Hungary and Iris, who at the time was single having divorced Count Gabor von Büdingen in 1927.

Paddy's next invitation came from Jăs and Clara Jelensky (*recte* Count Zselénszky de Zelanka) who lived in the 'low, ranch-like manor house of Tövisegyháza' ['Church of thorns']. According to Paddy, he was Polish from 'an excellent family in Southern Poland, eight thousand acres, not far from Cracow. His great-grandfather was Austrian ambassador to St. Petersburg and their Turk's head crest was granted for capturing three Tartar standards in the Ukraine'. She [a Zay de Csömör according to Paddy] was from the High Tatras whose family 'live in one of the most ancient castles in Hungary – Slovakia now, more's the pity! Counts since the reign of King Mátyás. They carry a double chevron dansetty between three salamanders quartered with five pikes haurient; arms parlant…after the river that rushes by, and the fish that swim in it[3].

There are two problems with this description. The first is that the Jelenskys did not live at Tövicsegyháza since the manor house there was the home of the Kintzig family. Apart from the clues of 'in a cornfield under a clump of elms' and 'chestnut trees along the edge of the lawn', there is little information as to the whereabouts of the house. In Zimandu Nou/Zimándújfalu, a village founded in 1852 by tobacco farmers who had been evicted from Csernovics-Ujfalu, there are records of the small village of Andrei Șaguna being established as a result of 'the dispossession of the Zselénszky manor' in 1921 owing to Romania's agrarian reforms.

The second puzzle is the Jelenskys themselves. Jas is a Pole from Cracow and Clara [or Klára Zay] is described as being of noble Hungarian birth although the use of the present tense – 'live' – does not help in identifying her family home for most of the castles in the High Tatras lie in ruins thanks to the prowess of the Austrian Emperor's engineers in blowing them up in the 17th and 18th centuries on the grounds they were rebel strongholds. The few that remained habitable either belonged to the Baron Thurzó de Bethlenfalva or Count Pálffy de Erdőd families. Both sets of arms are at odds with Paddy's description of salamanders and pike.

Intriguingly, there was a large mansion at Neudorf, across the Mureş river to the south of Maria Radna, which belonged to the old Polish family of Zselénszky de Zelanka[4]. Count Róbert Zselénszky [1850–1939], an active member of the Upper House of the Hungarian Parliament in Budapest and as a Vice President of the OMGE (National Economic

---

[3] *Between the Woods and the Water*

[4] Also known as Zelanka-Zelenski; and sometimes spelt as Zselinszky or Zsilinszky.

Association) an influential representative of his fellow landowners, also owned a *conac* near Utviniş. All this begs the question as to whether Jas Jelensky was not in fact a Zselénszky.

Neudorf was demolished after the Second World War and nothing remains of the great mansion.

Mounted on a horse lent to him by Clara, Paddy arrived at his next house party a few miles away at Scanteia/Tövisegyháza, this time as the guest of Janos Kintzig de Nyék[5]. The house had been built in 1903 as a wedding present by Janos for his fiancée, Erzsebet Beliczey de Bajcza. Paddy describes the family as Swabians which is misleading since it suggests that they were settlers who arrived in the Banat from the German-speaking lands in the early 18th century. The Kintzig family, originally from Würzburg, had lived in Schweinberg [equidistant between Munich and Salzburg] until the middle of the 18th century when they moved to Újszentanna in the county of Arad – not the Banat – and became members of the Hungarian minor nobility.

The daughter of the house, who looked like 'a fair-haired Englishwoman on safari', was 33-year-old Georgette Kintzig de Nyék. Although Paddy remembers her as 'striving for an annulment', she was in fact divorced from her husband, Graf Karl Sandor Hans Heinrich Anton Woracziczky von Pabienitz and was living at home in Tövisegyháza with her parents. The Woracziczky von Pabienitz family were certainly not Czechs as Paddy describes them. Dating back to 15th century in Pabienice in Poland, Karl's family were from the Bavarian Bissengen branch and he had been born in 1888 on his mother's family[6] estate at Mănăştur, a village equidistant between Arad and Timişoara.

The two Pallavicini brothers mentioned by Paddy were Tibor Solymossy's teenage nephews, János and Gábor, for his sister, Marta, was married to János Pallavicini[7], the son of Johann Markgraf von Pallavicini, one of the most prominent Imperial diplomats of the early 20th century. The 'nearby estate' is probably Ópusztaszeri near Szeged in Hungary, the imposing

---

[5] Paddy uses 'von' rather than 'de'.

[6] Reichsgräfin Khuen-Belasi from Poszony/Bratislava.

[7] Killed in action Warsaw July 1944

1910 home[8] of Count Sándor Pallavicini who had died the previous year. The Pallavicini boys lived at Pusztaradvány in the Zemplén Mountains in the north of Hungary.

The 'erudite naturalist landowner' and 'tall Princess' were the Anglophile[9] Baron Bela Lipthay de Kisfalud et Lubelle [1892–1974], a member of one of Hungary's oldest families dating back to the 13th century and best known as a famous lepidopterist, and his wife, Eugenia née Odescalchi de Szerem [1898–1985]. The wealthy Odescalchi siblings were much in demand; her sister married Baron Bánffy de Losoncz. At the time they lived at Lipthay kastély in Lovrin, a day's drive from Scanteia.

In contrast to the glamorous hostess of his last stop-over, the Friar Tuck-like figure of Brother Péter, the assistant guest-master of the Franciscan Abbey at Mănăstirea Maria Radna/Máriaradna, welcomed Paddy as a *viator* and, conversing in Latin, the two men enjoyed a game of skittles before attending Vespers and then dining in the refectory. Paddy dates the monastery at 1520, the year the first chapel was built, but a much earlier monastery and church had been commissioned in 1325 by Robert of Anjou, King of Hungary. After the Ottoman conquest of Timișoara in 1552, the monastery went into decline and it was only through the efforts of the enterprising Father Andrija Stipančić, who walked to Constantinople and back to secure a decree from the Sultan to repair it. In exchange for a large bribe, the chapel was restored.

In 1668, the friars acquired an icon of the Madonna printed by Remondini of Vicenza in his Bassano del Grappa workshop. Thirty years later, after Turkish soldiers had set fire to the chapel, the paper icon was found miraculously undamaged in the charred remains of what was left of the building. From then on, Maria Radna became a magnet for pilgrims, attracting so many people that a new and larger church and monastery had to be built in the 18th century. At Pentecost in 1767, more than 12,000 pilgrims from all over Europe attended the service. Fifty years later the number had risen to 25,000. In 1935, the year after Paddy's visit, more than 73,000 people made pilgrimages to Maria Radna, many of them on foot.

---

[8] The Pallavicinis had bought the estate in 1803 but their original mansion had been destroyed by the great flood of 1879 which inundated Szeged and the surrounding area. This splendid building is now a psychiatric hospital, much valued by the regional community.

[9] One of his tutors had been the talented New Zealand all-round sportsman Anthony Wilding, world tennis champion pre-1914.

Passing 'the tapering ruins of the castle of Solymos'[10], Paddy set off down the bucolic valley of the Mureş River, heading for kastély Konop, the country house of Mr. von Konopy with whom he had arranged to stay the night. This was probably an introduction from the Kintzig family for Georgette's maternal grandmother was a Konopi de Konop[11]. He inadvertently passed it and hitched a ride back down the road on a hay-waggon. Mr. von Konopi was in fact Kálmán Konopi de Konop, a Hungarian nobleman whose family had owned the kastély and the 2,000-hectare estate at Odvoş/Konop since the 17th century.

The last surviving member of the Konopi family, Kálmán (1880–1947) was an engineer and agronomist. Famous as the inventor of the three Odvoşi wheat varieties, wheat breeding was his life's work, certainly not a hobby to which Paddy consigned it!

'It might have been a rural deanery' wrote Paddy, a comparison that implies the wealth of the Church of England rather than the modest circumstances of the lesser Hungarian nobility. Nevertheless, the kastély/manor was a substantial country house with an imposing portico supported by four columns.

As he crossed the Mureş to his south, Paddy correctly reflected that 'although this region was Transylvanian in feeling, strictly speaking it was the north-easternmost corner of the old Banat of Temesvár'. His new host was Count Jenő Teleki de Szék [1881–1947], a cousin of Pál Teleki, the former Prime minister of Hungary whom Paddy had met in Budapest. The Telekis were one of the great Hungarian houses of Transylvania, their main estates straddling the Mureş at Târgu Mureş/ Marosvásárhely some 200 miles upstream from this remote corner of the Banat.

It was somewhat tactless of Count Jenő to describe the 'petite Trianon' mansion at Căpâlnaş/ Kápolnás as 'only early 19th century and perhaps a bit showy' for it actually belonged to the family of his wife Ecaterina ['Katinka'], the Mocsonyis de Foen[12] who were neither Hungarian

---

[10] The former stronghold of the 15th century Moravian mercenary, Jan Jiskra z Brandýsa, one of the outstanding soldiers of his era. Its Romanian name is Şoimoş.

[11] Originally Czigler de Konop.

[12] http://ploaiadecuvinte.blogspot.co.uk/2012/05/personalitati-banatene-familia-mocioni.html

nor Transylvanian but Aromanians, originally from Thessaly and then Moscopole in Ottoman Albania[13]. Petru Mocsonyi *aliter* Popovich had served with Prince Eugene of Savoy at the Battle of Zenta in 1697 and thus the family started a long and profitable relationship with Vienna which culminated in their ennoblement as Barons Mocsonyi de Foen in 1783. All the properties of the Bulci line to which Katinka [1883–1959][14] was related were situated in the Banat – the castles of Bulci, Birchiş, and Căpâlnaş on the south bank of the Mureş valley i.e. the old border between the Banat and Transylvania, Foeni south west of Timişoara and Vlaicovăţ[15] which ended up in post-Trianon Serbia [Vlajkovac].

Ionel Mocsonyi had bought the land at Căpâlnaş, for the princely sum of 260,000 florins from the Zichy family in 1853. His son Mihai [1811–90] and his spouse, Ecaterina Mocsonyi de Foen, who was also his cousin, then commissioned the Viennese architect, Otto Koloman Wagner, to build a new castle for them in the historicist style in 1876. It soon became famous for its musical soirées as their son Eugen and daughter-in-law Terezia Horváth de Zalabér were both accomplished pianists[16]

Paddy described his host as 'a tall, spreading, easy-going, middle-aged man, with gold-rimmed spectacles and a remarkably intelligent, slightly ugly and very amusing face' and his hostess as 'tall, dark-haired, fine-looking, very kind and very intelligent'. Life at the house revolved around the library from where Count Jenő masterminded his world-class collection of moths, a hobby very much in the traditions of this great Transylvanian family of polymaths, bibliophiles, explorers and politicians.

Frederic König, a well-known lepidopterist from Timişoara, was invited by the count in 1936 to come over and help him arrange his collection of over 25,000 beetles and insects. On his first day at Căpâlnaş, after viewing the collection, he set off with his host to collect specimens in the forest. 'The peasants on the way greeted us with a respectful lifting of the straw hat. We met a wagon loaded with wood. The count smiled and said "Look how he's trying to hide behind his wagon but I know who he is! But there's still enough wood to go around..."'. That evening, the castle courtyard, covered up to the first floor with a glass ceiling, was transformed into an elegant dining room with a mosaic parquet floor of different varieties of wood. The centerpiece was a table about 10 meters long, with each dish and glass placed on a fine Chinese straw mat. König remembered 'two

---

[13] Mocsopole – Voskopojë – is outside of Korçë.

[14] Her three brothers, Petru, Alexandru and Ionel, had all died unmarried.

[15] Now the property of the Bissingen-Nippenburg family after restitution.

[16] Teodor Botiş.

nicely dressed girls came in and filled the dishes, first with soup, then with the next course'.

Beneath the jovial surface of this eccentric household lay a tragic story. Covering the castle's roof, there was what the Romanians call a '*luminator*', a large rectangular glass structure that was replicated by a similar glass awning on the first floor, both of which allowed light to illuminate the corridors and percolate into the recesses which led off the open-space quadrangular design. The Teleki's 3-year-old daughter, Eduardina ['Mády'], is said to have fallen over the banisters when running down a corridor and died after crashing into the well through the glass window.

Her brother Jenő was born the year she died and would have been about 12 at the time of Paddy's stay. In *Between the Woods and the Water*, he notes that 'there was a nice looking, rather spoiled son called Michael [Eugen[17] "Bubi" Teleki] and his Hungarian tutor at the castle, and a moving population of visitors; and one was aware of the Countess's recently invalid mother[18] in one wing of the building'. She died when Paddy was staying with his friend Elemér further up the valley and he described how they took a train 'flying a pale feather of smoke and looking like a toy among the trees and the hills' to Căpâlnaș in time for the funeral 'held in the hall' where three Uniat priests intoned the rites in Romanian.

From Căpâlnaș, Paddy accompanied the Telekis to lunch at Săvârşin/ Soborsin, a pretty yellow ochre Maria Theresa-style Neo-Classical country house set in a twenty-hectare park above the River Mureş. Built in 1650 by the Brunswik von Korompa family who had received the domain as a gift from the Austrian Emperor, it passed through the female line to the Forray family when Julie Brunswik married Count Forray de Soborsin and then in 1852 it once again passed through the female line, this time to count Nádasdy de Nádasd et Fogarasföld family. Burnt down twice, first during the uprising of Horea, Cloşca and Crişan in 1784 and then during the Revolution of 1848, the Nádasdys employed an Austrian architect to add a new storey and design the Neo-Classical side wings.

That was not the end of the ownership line. In 1941, the sole heir of the family, Count Ferenc Hunyady de Kéthely [1895–1966], who was married to Julia Nádasdy, became Minister of the Interior of Hungary, a position which excluded him from owning properties in Romania. So he made a

---

[17] Jenő is Eugen in German.

[18] This was the 75-year-old Therezia Mocsonyi who died in 1934 after Paddy's departure.

deal with his neighbour, Count Antoniu de Mocsonyi, and swopped the Castle of Săvârşin for a Mocsonyi property near Budapest.

When Queen Elena of Romania first visited Săvârşin, she fell in love with it and, as a gesture of appreciation towards the Royal Family, Count Antoniu, who was also the godfather of King Michael I, sold it to him for a modest sum in 1942[19]. Out of earshot from Bucharest, Săvârşin and the neighbouring Mocsonyi mansion at Bulci became the secret settings for the young King's plot to remove Marshal Antonescu from power and to take Romania out of the war. In January 1948, after the King had been coerced into abdicating by the Soviet Union's Romanian puppets, Groza and Gheoghiu-Dej, the castle was nationalized and remained government property until 2001 when it was returned to its rightful owners, the Romanian royal family.

Paddy's host at Săvârşin, Count Ferenc Hunyady, was a leading figure in the Smallholders Party and lived mainly in Budapest. In 1935, the party won 20% of the vote which gave it 22 seats in the National Assembly, the second largest party but a fraction of the size of the Party of National Unity with 164 seats. His house guest, Baron Gábor Apor de Altorja [1889–1969] who was the permanent deputy of the Minister of Foreign Affairs at the time, came from one of Transylvania's oldest families that had arrived with the first wave of Székelys. The exact date of their arrival remains contentious: most Hungarian historians subscribe to the timeline that the Székely were in Erdély (Transylvania) already prior to the 9th century conquest of Pannonia by the Magyars. It is Romanian historians who write that the Székelys arrived later in the 13th century and this differentiation continues today although post-Ceauşescu there are also Romanian historians who agree that the Székelys arrived in Erdély around the same time as the Magyars in Pannonia proper[20]. Later Baron Gábor became Hungarian Minister at the Holy See from 1939 to 1944. His ancestor, Baron Péter Apor wrote a memoir in 1736, bemoaning the changes in Transylvania from 'the wealth of its simple modest times to the penury of its present haughty, extravagant and demented estate'. The *Metamorphosis Transylvaniae* remains one of the most endearing and funniest books written about Transylvania.

The Hunyadys de Kéthely had been created counts in Hungary in 1792; their estates to the South of Lake Balaton were famous for horse and sheep

---

[19] When he succeeded Count Anton in 1943 and inherited his estates, Baron Ionel gave the young King several thousand acres of forestry to the NE and SE of Săvârşin.

[20] 2017 Author's correspondence with Tötösy de Zepetnek, Steven.

breeding as well as for the wines from Kéthely. Ferenc's father, Károly, who had died the previous year, had been a regular officer in the Nádasdy Regiment and had retired to his wife's [Julia Irma Nádasdy de Nádasd et Fogarasföld] estate at Săvârşin after the Treaty of Trianon. With the estate no longer part of Hungary, he learnt Romanian and set about managing the 5,000 acres of forest and arable land together with a major timber company that belonged to the estate. His passion was hunting and in the forests surrounding the house a system of telephones was set up to report on the movement of game – wild boar, deer and bears.

The cousin of Countess Tinka who lived at Bulci/Bulcs was Count Antoniu de Mocsonyi[21]. 'With a high-bridged nose and receding chin, fif-tyish, cosmopolitan, urbane and clever, he was an excellent shot, and King Carol[22] had appointed him Grand Veneur du Roi, or Master of the Royal Hunt; the position involved game, beaters and shooting rather than horses and hounds.'[23] The castle at Bulci, built in Neo-Classical style in the early 19th century by Baron Fechtig de Fechtenberg[24], had been bought by the Mocsonyi family in 1858 and was a favourite weekend haunt of Bucharest politicians.

In *The Broken Road*, Paddy refers to him as a 'Hungarian magnate in Transylvania' who had broken out the self-imposed isolation of 'other Transylvanian landowners'. Uncharacteristically, given his passion for the particular, in this instance Paddy wrongly lumps Transylvania and the Banat together although he was correct in thinking that the Romanians of the former Banat held the Mocsonyi family in high esteem. In *Between the Woods and the Water*, he correctly summarizes that 'the Countess's ancestors [i.e. Mocsonyis] …remembered their origins and supported Rumanian aspirations. Magyar may have been their earliest language

---

[21] Mocioni in Romanian.

[22] He wrongly attributes his appointment to King Carol. It was in fact King Ferdinand who appointed him [Notes by Baron Ionel Mocsonyi-Styrcea by kind permission Michael de Styrcea].

[23] *Between the Woods and the Water.*

[24] Baron Ferdinand married Countess Cassis-Faraone from a wealthy Trieste merchant family. Her father, a former general tax collector for the Bey of Egypt, had the idea of buying horses directly in the Arab countries and then selling them in Europe. The Baron took it on and the first horses arrived around 1810. Soon his customers included the Kings of Württemberg and Bavaria as well as the Emperor of Austria.

for generations; but, as MPs, they always held heterodox views in the Budapest parliament'. The descriptor 'magnate' is more usually associated with the Magnates' Conspiracy of 1670 when Counts Rákóczi, Nádasdy and Zrinyi, all holders of high state office, were arrested for plotting rebellion against the Emperor.

In 1848, when it looked like the Habsburg Empire was about to unravel as revolution swept through Europe, the Banat Romanians, like the Transylvania Romanians at Blaj, had gathered in great numbers outside the town of Lugoş to articulate their demands for autonomy. However, without the military resources of the Hungarians who had openly rebelled against their Austrian masters, the Banat Romanians had to play their hand with great skill and by adopting a cautious strategy of non-violence and moderation deftly avoided the wrath visited on the rebellious Hungarians by the Emperor's Russian allies. However, after the *Ausgleich*, that great political rapprochement between Austria and Hungary, Ferenc Deák's Nationality Law of December 1868 was passed by the Hungarian Parliament. In essence it denied the legal existence of the non-Magyar nations by recognizing only Hungary and thus ensuring its legal supremacy over all the others.

It was at this point that Andrei Mocsonyi, one of the twenty-five Romanian deputies who took their seats in the parliament in Budapest, voiced his concern about the rabid nature of nationalism and he pleaded eloquently in favour of racial equality and compromise. This was not the first time he had clashed with Hungarian nationalists for he had been a longtime supporter of an autonomous Banat, be it a Dukedom or Captaincy, within the Empire. His plea went unheeded at the time but by standing up to Budapest, he became an icon for Romanian self-determination. His nephew, the politician Alexandru Mocsonyi, was also a champion of self-determination. With these family credentials, Count Antoniu Mocsonyi de Foen was openly accepted by the ruling Romanian elite in Bucharest in a manner which would have been politically impossible if he had been a pure Transylvanian Hungarian e.g. a Bánffy or Teleki. As a prominent supporter of the People's Party, Count Antoniu had had the ear of Alexandru Averescu during his three terms as Prime Minister in the 1920s.

Eight years later, during the summer of 1944, Bulci became the nucleus of resistance to the Antonescu regime. Count Antoniu's adopted son, the highly intelligent Cambridge-educated Baron Ionel de Mocsonyi-Stârcea, became head of Chancery to Rosetti-Solescu, the Marshal of the Court, and three months later in August 1942, when Solescu left, he was made acting Marshal[25]. In the coup against Prime Minister ["Conducator"] Ion Antonescu in August 1944, it was Baron Ionel who detained him and locked him up in the safe containing the King's stamp collection. He went on to become a leading organizer of the National Resistance Movement in a forlorn attempt to prevent the Communist Party taking power. Consequently, he was arrested, put on trial and spent the next 15 years in Securitate jails, where he was badly tortured and spent the majority of his imprisonment in solitary confinement. In 1962, he was released and lived in Switzerland until his death in 1992. For much of that time he assisted the exiled King Michael and dedicated his life to the restoration of the monarchy and a free Romania.

The other guests who came over to Săvârşin with the Bulci house party were Gregoire Duca, brother of the Prime Minister Ion Duca, who had been assassinated six months earlier by the Iron Guard as he stepped off a train at Sinaia station. The daughter of the former Foreign Minister who had attended the Paris Peace Conference, could be either a Bratiănu, Mişu, Vaida-Voevod or Zamfirescu. The trouble is that none of her husband's surnames fit Paddy's billing for having been shot in the stomach in a duel! The passionate and famous lady bridge player alas remains unidentified and Josias von Rantzau, First Secretary at the German Legation, reappears later in Paddy's journal when he reached Bucharest.

The scion of one of the oldest families in Schleswig Holstein, 31-year-old Josias von Rantzau had been posted to Bucharest in 1933 after his first *Auswärtiges Amt* appointment in Stockholm where he had been Head of the Economics Department. His father had been the Oberhofmarschall[26] in Mecklenburg-Schwerin when Schleswig Holstein was still a province of Prussia and when the Grand Duke abdicated in 1918, it was Ceno von Rantzau who negotiated the terms for the free State of Mecklenburg-Schwerin. Josias left Bucharest in January 1936 to become vice-consul in the German Consul General in New York and it was here that he met the future opponent of the Nazi state, Adam von Trott zu Solz. While there is no evidence that he was an active member of the *Kreisauer Kreis*, by all accounts Josias like many of his aristocratic *Auswärtiges Amt* contemporaries, made a reluctant Nazi.

From the USA, he was sent to London as legation secretary at the German embassy where he remained until the declaration of war in 1939. After a stint as the *Auswärtiges Amt* representative at OKW [the German

---

[25] He was made Marshal of the Court on 23 August 1994 until he resigned om grounds of ill-health on 4 November 1944.

[26] Chief of the court and Marshal's office in Schwerin.

High Command][27], he returned to Bucharest in April 1943 as head of the Department of Culture with an additional brief for the German Scientific Institute in Bucharest. On 14 January 1944, he became First Councilor but when the Red Army occupied Bucharest in September, he was arrested by SMERSH, the Soviet Counter-Intelligence arm[28], and taken along with other Bucharest-based German diplomats to Moscow where he was imprisoned in the infamous Lefortovo prison. At an unknown time, he was transferred to the No. 58 War Crimes Camp, where he probably died in June 1950. On 31 August 1951 he was officially declared dead in Germany[29].

About 10 miles due east of Săvârşin, Paddy made his 'first real Transylvanian halt' at Castelul Nopcsa at Zam, set on a bend in the Mureş river. Here he met 'the thirty-year-old' Xenia Csernovics[30] de Mácsa et Kis-Oroszi, 'the kastély-dweller' with 'something arresting and unforgettable about her ivory complexion and raven hair and sloe-black eyes'. She was in fact only 25 years old and lived at Zam with her widowed mother, Gerda [née von Prokopovics[31]], and three sisters, Laura, Roza and Constansia[32]. Xenia was the only one married – her husband was Gábor Betegh de Csíktusnád, who came from an old Székely family at Băile Tuşnad. They had two children, Gábor, who was later killed in 1945 and Maria, who married Count Mihály Teleki de Szék in 1958 [they had two sons, László and Gábor]. As to whether Paddy had an affair with her remains unclear. Michael O'Sullivan suggests that 'the balance of probability, in the seduction stakes, most likely rests with his success…'[33]

Zam, although a substantial property, was a modest manor compared to the great family mansion at Macea [Mácsa], which, along with its

---

[27] See correspondence Von Rantzau-Hans Alexander Winkler, *Auswärtiges Amt* representative with Afrika Korps [Jeffrey Hert, Nazi Propaganda for the Arab World, YUP 2009].

[28] Vadim Birstein: *Smersh: Stalin's Secret Weapon*, Biteback, 2013

[29] Tatiana von Metternich-Winneburg: *Bericht eines ungewöhnlichen Lebens*. Goldmann, München 1976.

[30] Also spelt Csernovits and Čarnojević.

[31] Her mother's family were the Dadányis de Gyülvész, ennobled by Emperor Franz I in 1808.

[32] Her eldest brother Arzen died in 1961 and her other brothers, the twins Pal and Ivan, died at the relatively young ages of 33 and 36.

[33] https://patrickleighfermor.org/2014/11/25/angelas-fate/

magnificent botanical gardens and vast estate, Xenia's great grandfather Péter Csernovics [1813–92] had lost to the Károlyi family in a card game. There is an additional element of sadness to this story for twenty years before, Péter's wife, Laura, had died at the young age of 32, leaving him with an 11-year-old son, Arsenije [Xenia's grandfather], and three daughters, aged five, two and one. By a judicious marriage to a Serbian heiress, Ružica Anastasijevic, who was related to 'The Prince of the Danube' Captain Misa Anastasijevic, who had made a fortune out of shipping salt, Arsenije managed to restore some of the family fortune.

Paddy missed the significance of Castelul Nopcsa for in the story of the house and its owners the timeless political dilemma of Transylvanian is ensconced. Since the 13th century, the Nopcea family, one of the oldest in Transylvania, had lived there. As Orthodox Christians, they had fought on the side of the Hungarian King at the battle of Nicopolis in 1396, the equivalent in terms of English prestige of fighting for Harold at Hastings. Later related by marriage to the great Janos Hunyadi, their arms displayed a blazon with a decapitated Turk's head and a raven with a ring in its mouth [a Hunyadi device]. In 1701, when Transylvania had become a province of Austria, one branch of the family converted to Catholicism which gave them the right to be representatives at the Transylvanian Diet. Their name became magyarised to Nopcsa

With such impeccable Imperial and Hungarian credentials, it came as a surprise when László [Vasile in Romanian] Nopcsa de Felső-Szilvás, the supreme commander of Hunedoara County for over 15 years, attended the Romanian National Assembly at Blaj in May 1848 where Transylvanian Romanians had gathered to protest against the unification with Hungary demanded by Kossuth, the leader of the Hungarian nationalist party. The assembly went further and requested that the Austrian constitution be applied in Transylvania for Austria, it argued, should become 'a free association of free nations.' It called for a provisional government that included Romanians as well as Saxons and Hungarians, and demanded that a diet be convened to take decisions on Transylvania's future.

László's appearance at Blaj so incensed the Transylvanian Hungarians that on 3 November that year, Hungarian revolutionaries attacked Zam where Romanian border guards were stationed. The kastély was to all extents demolished. Nopcsa, by now an outcast, withdrew from public life. His crime had been to put the long-term interests of Transylvania before Hungarian hegemony. Yet within the space of a year, the Hungarian independence movement had been brutally crushed; László 's sons went on to serve as Chancellor to the Empress Sisi and as a commander of

Archduke Maximilian's Guards in Mexico. With their main seat at Săcel[34] in Hunedoara county, the family received the title of Barons of the Imperial Court in 1855[35].

The ruins of Castelul Nopcsa at Zam were bought in 1879 by Dr Lekisch, a Viennese lawyer, who erected a new mansion on the site. In turn, he sold it to Count Mihaly Czernovics who is credited with creating the impressive park with its exotic trees and plants. There is a mysterious story about the Count, who supposedly discovered a map of old tunnels linking Zam with the castle at Deva. He would invite his guests to explore this subterranean labyrinth where they were either robbed or killed by a predatory figure wearing a black velvet mask. Unfortunately, the count's archive went up in flames in 1948, so there is no trace of the map but the ghost of the cavernous bandit is said to still stalk the *kastély*. Those who ask the spectre where his [or maybe her] treasure is are said to end up either in the River Mureş or in front of the express train that passes by the kastély as it hurtles through the valley!

Gurasada/ Guraszáda, 8 miles to the east of Zam, was Paddy's penultimate stop-over in the Mureş valley before he made his way south to the Danube. This 'mixture of manor house, monastery and farmstead' was the home of 'István' Elemér Klobusiczky de Klobusicz et Zétény[36] and his parents, whose family had been ennobled by Maria Theresa. The 18th century family seat, kastély Klobušiczhý at Tarcaszentpéter[37] [Petrovany in today's Slovakia], had passed through marriage to Count Szirmay de Szirma et Szirmabesenyő family in the late 19th century, leaving Elemér's line 'with little actual cash about, but plenty of everything else'.

When Paddy and István returned from their trip with 'Angela' [the name Paddy had chosen to disguise the identity of Xenia Csernovics] around

---

[34] Their other country houses were at Zam, Fărcădin and Densuş and their town house in Arad.

[35] Laszlo's grandson, Baron Ferenc Nopcsa de Felső-Szilvás, made a name for himself as an adventurer, scholar, and paleontologist. He is widely regarded as one of the founders of paleobiology and Albanian studies. At one point, he put his name forward as King for the newly independent Albania but was turned down on account of his homosexuality.

[36] Paddy again uses 'von' rather than 'de'.

[37] See https://www.youtube.com/watch?v=9C5RFeAiyec.

Transylvania at the end of July, they handed the car they had borrowed back to its owner, Lázár, who lived on the south bank of the Mureş at Lăpuşnic, 3 miles away from Gurasada. Here Paddy stayed for two days, enjoying the company of Lázár and Elemér and another neighbour from nearby Illia/Marosillye[38], István Horváth, before setting off on his own to Tomeşti/ Csíkszenttamás where he arrived at nightfall as the guest of Herr Robert von Winkler, 'a tall thin scholarly man, living alone with his books and guns on the steep edge of the forest'. Paddy presents him as a strange scholar-hunter, 'he and his library a treasure-house of relevant knowledge'. The stairs were 'forested with horns, antlers, fowling-pieces and wolf-traps…the skins of two enormous wolves on the landing, a stuffed lynx on the wall, a row of boars' tushes and a bear's skin on my bedroom floor'. In reality, Winkler was a failed businessman.

Through marriage to the grand-daughter of Josif Losch, an Austrian whose family had acquired a glass-making factory in Tomeşti from a Hungarian entrepreneur, Anton Pfantzels, in 1846, Winkler had become the proprietor of the Tomeschter Glashütte. Despite the abundance of wood for the furnaces, water and raw materials, over the years the business often found it hard to compete. In the late 19th century, Josif had managed to attract foreign specialists by building housing and a school but labour always remained a problem in this remote wild part of the Banat. Winkler himself oversaw the construction of sixty workers' homes, together with the introduction of a common bakery and communal farm animals. In 1928, buoyed by a strong order book, he built a second furnace and acquired additional forests for fuel. Then came the 1929 crash, quickly followed by the depression. It proved a disaster.

Unable to pay wages and suppliers for several months, in 1931 Winkler was forced to cede the company to the National Credit Society of Bucharest which relaunched it as the Cooperative Glass Factory of Tomeşti. By the time Paddy arrived, the family business was no more and his host no longer the all-powerful local industrialist. The fact that he had stayed on in the village suggests that he had retained the respect of the workforce for his philanthropic work practices and his efforts to keep the business afloat.

The approach to Băile Herculane is dramatic as the sides of the valley of the River Cerna contract and soar up like the spires and towers of Gothic

---

[38] The village has two significant buildings – the Red Bastion [Veres Bástya], probably the first Italian-designed bastion in Transylvania c.1640, and the mid 19th century Bornemissza kastély.

cathedrals, becoming sheer limestone cliffs that mysteriously capture the sun's fading rays. After about three miles, the old town appears and the haunt of Emperors, both Roman and Habsburg, Kings and Queens, Princes and boyars, magnates and burghers, and English vagabonds is revealed.

John Paget in his 1860 journey to Transylvania warned of *ennui* following the *de rigeur* parboil and the 'deficiency of accommodation …a crying evil…new arrivals not infrequently are obliged to sleep on tables and chairs in the public dining room'. Seventy years later, Paddy passed through this 'ornate and incongruous watering-place' which he imagined once had been a haunt of 'ailing burghers of Eastern Europe, in crinolines and stove pipe hats, sabretaches and czapkas, or mutton-chop sleeves and boaters'.

Paddy's host was Herr Heinz Schramm, a 'cheerful and rubicund schoolmate' of Elemér. He lived outside the town in a large and comfortable house with his father, a retired Admiral in the Austrian Imperial Navy.

In this 'echo of the Austrian-Hungarian Empire at its farthest edge', Paddy and Heinz drove into town for a gala night. As the evening 'spun itself into a golden haze', he danced with a girl studying English in Bucharest to the tunes of *Couchés dans le foin* and *Vous qui passez sans me voir*.

For Romanians, Paddy presents in *Between the Woods and the Water* a curious sympathetic cameo of disenfranchised Hungarian nobility and landed gentry stripped of their privileges and shorn of much of their land. He completely overlooks the irreducible fact that Austria-Hungary had been an enemy of Romania in the First World War, the Hungarians alone providing the Royal Hungarian Honvéd of 7 infantry divisions and 10 cavalry divisions as part of the 3 million strong Austro-Hungary army[39]. Romania's half a million total military and civilian losses represented a catastrophic 8% of her population and ranked second highest to those of Serbia [16%]. He compounds this strange oversight by perversely insisting on referring to former Hungarian cities and towns by their Hungarian names. With his youthful English susceptibility to class hierarchy and impressed by 'noblemen of all sorts', the young Paddy was looking at the world of Romania in 1934 through the hazy lens of Imperial yesteryear.

---

[39] Many Romanians living in Transylvania and the Bucovina found themselves conscripted into the Austro-Hungarian army. Their losses were in the region of 150,000.

Fifty years later, after years of selective editing and by now a senior member of the English chapter of the contemporary *Ordo Vagorum*, Paddy was determined to remain faithful to these youthful impressions save for an admissive line in *The Broken Road* when he acknowledges that 'during all this immense tract of time [from the 13th to 20th century when the Saxons, Hungarians and Székelys ruled Transylvania] the Rumanians, who outnumbered all the others put together and now ruled the country, had not only had no say in running Transylvania but no official existence at all...'

Josias von Rantzau

Baron Gábor Apor

Count Jenő Teleki

Countess Tinka Teleki

Count Bubi Teleki

Countess Therezia Mocsonyi

Count Antoniu Mocsonyi

Baron Ionel Mocsonyi-Stârcea

King Michael of Romania at Bulci

Hunting lunch at Bulci

L to R: The garden terrace at Bulci – Queen Anne of Romania, Baron Ionel Mocsonyi – Stârcea, Queen Elena of Romania [the Queen Mother], 'Biellie' Mocsonyi-Stârcea, N/K, King Michael of Romania

L to R: The Hunting Lodge at Bulci – King Michael of Romania, Queen Elena of Romania, Bielle Mocsonyi-Stârcea, Baron Ionel Mocsonyi-Stârcea, Grigore Niculescu-Buzesti, N/K, butler

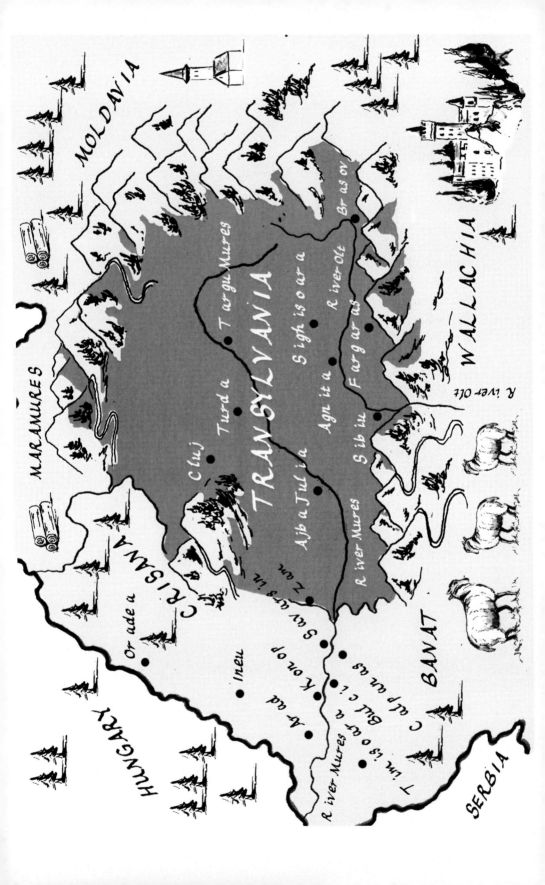

THE SECRET JOURNEY
[Place names in Romanian, Hungarian and German]

'…a vertiginous triangle of steep roofs, spikes, tree-tops and battlemented cliffs rose like a citadel in an illuminator psalter.'

⁓Between the Woods and the Water

An enduring mystery of Paddy's first journey through Romania in *Between the Woods and the Water* is whether the 'secret journey to the interior of Transylvania' in Elemér's borrowed 'well-polished blue touring car' ever took place for the errors and omissions are legion.

Alba Iulia/ Gyulafehérvár/Karlsburg

The great János Hunyadi, whose fortress Paddy had visited with the Telekis at Hunedoara, and his son László are described by Paddy as 'entombed under the vaults' in the 13th century St. Michael's Cathedral at Alba Iulia. Technically this is may be correct but surely any visitor would be impressed by their magnificent marble sarcophagi embellished with carved reliefs of hard-won battles and the polished figures which lie on top in the traditional stony repose of medieval knights. Furthermore, there are three Hunyadis lying alongside each other, for János's younger brother is also here.

Paddy has ignored the magnificent setting of Giovanni Visconti's early 18th century Vauban-style 'Alba Carolina' fortress in which the Cathedral and Bishop's Palace sit. With its seven prominent bastions protruding like giant spikes into the landscape, the fortress is one of the Baroque glories of Transylvania

He also missed the grandiose Church of National Unity, built in 1921 in the Brâncoveanu national revival style. With its shady belvederes, elegant loggias and well laid out gardens, it was the scene of the Coronation of King Ferdinand and Queen Marie in 1922.

The idea of a coronation had been mooted soon after the First World War peace settlements, but with no consensus among the bickering political parties, Ferdinand and Marie declined to participate. The Church at Alba Iulia thus stood empty. When Brătianu, the architect of Greater Romania, was re-elected Prime Minister in 1922, the Royal couple agreed to a ceremony. Yet the event was still beset with problems: the Transylvanians refused to take part and the Catholic Church forbade the King [who was an RC] from being crowned by an Orthodox priest in a Romanian Church. The latter difficulty was neatly sidestepped by Queen Marie who proposed an outdoor ceremony and for the King to crown himself. She took on the project with her unique sense of theatricality and flair for design.

On the day, after a private Mass, the Royal couple emerged from the Church and were led by the bishops onto a dais before a crowd of 300,000. Under a canopy held aloft by six giant spears, Ferdinand crowned himself with the iron crown of his uncle, King Carol the First, made out of a Turkish canon which he had personally captured at the Battle of Pleven in 1867. The King then turned to Marie, supplicant on her knees, and placed on her head a huge gold crown, set with rubies, emeralds, turquoises and moonstones, a copy of Lady Elena-Despina's headdress in her marriage to Neagoe Basarab, ruler of Walachia between 1512 and 1521. Surrounded by the Royal ladies dressed in gold and courtiers in mauve and silver, this was a glorious sight from Medieval times as had been Marie's intention. The guns roared, bells rang and a huge cheer went up from the crowd.

All this had happened a mere twelve years before Paddy visited Alba Iulia. Elemér and 'Angela' would surely have discussed it, even if as Hungarians they may have chosen not to attend it.

Paddy's history of Transylvania in this section is prone to error. In 1711, Transylvania was not 'once more part of Hungary'; it was an Austrian province ruled directly by Vienna for the Emperor Leopold had tightened his grip on Transylvania. After meeting with Miklós Bethlen, the representative of the Transylvanian Diet, he issued the Diploma Leopoldinum on 16 October 1690, reaffirming the privileges of the three *nati*[1] and the special position of the accepted religions, within the framework of an autonomous province that reported directly to Vienna. There was to be no reunification of Transylvania with Hungary. He rejected the elections as Prince of both Thököly, the Ottoman nominee, and Mihály II Apafi, the Diet's nominee, and introduced an independent civil administration. The Diet swore an oath of allegiance to Leopold.

The same went for the Banat – it too became an Austrian province – for the Habsburgs were still fearful of unrest in the East which had bedeviled their relations with the Hungarians since the Magnates' Conspiracy of 1664. The political wounds of the Thököly and Rákóczi rebellions still festered.

The location of a busy market 'down a side turning a few miles further north' [of Alba Iulia] is perplexing, for markets are usually in towns in this part of the world. Occasionally a Saint's Day attracts crowds to a remote church or monastery. Is this an oblique reference to the Mount Gaina 'girl fair'? Alas, there is no jagged skyline to the western mountain-mass of the old principality; the prospect is that of an outline of huge hills which comprise the Apuseni Mountains overlapping one another as they stretch west into Hungary.

Turda/Torda/Thorenburg

The famous underground salt mine at Turda, which since the 13th century had been a source of considerable wealth for Transylvania's owners, had been closed in 1932, a major talking point at the time. Paddy's statement that they were 'worked to this day by convicts' is totally wrong. Prisoners were never used as the workforce in the Turda Salt Mine; indeed this was the case throughout Transylvania. Salt cutters were traditionally hired for one year, with their contract being signed on 7 January. As a group, they received a barrel of wine, an ox and 100 loaves of bread on the four major celebrations of Christmas, Easter, Ascension Day, and All Saints Day[2].

---

[1] The three political constituencies of Transylvania – Saxons, Hungarians and Székelys.

[2] www.salinaturda.eu.

No mention is made of Turda's Roman heritage – the baths, the Milliarium milestone of Aiton, and Potaissa camp, home of Legio V Macedonica, one of the original twenty-eight legions raised by Octavian in the 1st century BC.

Cluj/Kolosvár/Klausenburg

The town houses – 'their owners away for the harvest' – were never occupied in the summer months. The great families descended on Cluj and other such towns in late October for the winter season of balls, gambling, theatre and opera. Oddly, Paddy refers to this in the previous paragraph.

In 1934 the Bánffy Palace was the town house of Count Miklós Bánffy, not a museum as it is today[3]. How did Paddy's little group manage to 'have a quick look at…the books and treasures'? If they were trying to keep Xenia under wraps and their visit a secret, it seems unlikely that Elemér would have asked Count Miklós if they could drop in.

The road to Târgu Mureş/Marosvásárhely/Neumarkt

Their route by car to Târgu Mureş in 1934 would have either been southwards back to Turda and then along the road to Luduş where they would have rejoined the River Mureş and headed East. If this was the case, they would have passed the former Bethlen mansion at Iernut, lost in a card game by its owner in 1885 to Eugene Haller who then gave it to the church, and the magnificent Haller mansion at Sânpaul, one of the great country houses of Transylvania at the time. The other route would have been to drive East and then either turn South towards Sârmaşu and Luduş or, more likely, to Satu Nou and then South East. On any of these routes, 'dark canyons' are not to be found.

Târgu Mureş

The reference to 'a huge church' in the market place of this bustling Hungarian town can only be the newly constructed [started 1925] The Ascension of the Lord Orthodox Cathedral. The iconostasis was still being painted in 1934! This monumental building with its political overtones of post-First World War Romanian Orthodox supremacy deliberately dominates the open space once presided over by the great 15th century Reformed Church in the Fortress – at one time a Franciscan monastery – and the typically Baroque 18th century RC Church of St John the Baptist with its putti-crowded interior and the nearby Baroque Grey Friars Church, another Franciscan endowment.

---

[3] It was nationalized in 1951 by the City authorities as an art gallery.

Similar cathedrals were erected in Cluj and in Timișoara though the latter, the largest of them all with its 300 feet tower, does not intrude on Union Square where the Roman Catholic and Serbian Orthodox Cathedrals still harmoniously face one another. In the Saxon strongholds, an accommodation had been reached much earlier; the grand copy of Constantinople's Saint Sophia was completed in Sibiu in 1904 and the Orthodox Cathedral in Brasov nearly ten years earlier.

No mention is made of architects Marcell Komor and Dezső Jakabs and their brilliant *gesamtkunstwerk*, the spectacular Palace of Culture [1910] with its mirrored hall and Miksa Roth's richly coloured stained glass windows of haunting Székelys folk tales or indeed the vividly decorated city hall [1905], both spectacular examples of a hybrid of Hungarian Art Nouveau, Arts and Crafts and Secessionist architecture. Together these buildings dominate the Western end of the market place.

Nor is a word said about the beautiful Baroque Teleki library, one of the first [1802] libraries in Europe. Later Paddy writes 'we had clean forgotten to look at the Teleki library'. Since he had not looked at any other buildings other than the 'huge church', this strikes one as a somewhat selective confession.

Sighişoara/Segesvár/Schäßburg

Founded by Saxons in the mid twelfth century, Sighişoara was first documented in 1280 as *Castrum Sex* – Castle Number Six – and known as the Rothenburg[4] of Transylvania.

No mention is made by Paddy of the Guilds that sponsored the fourteen towers that surround the town [nine still stand]. The 'hands of an old clock over an archway' is a scant description of the majestic 14th century double barbican clock tower that rises 200 feet to dominate the old town and the surrounding countryside. Curious Baroque wooden figurines emerge by the clock-face to mark the hour and announce the day.

'We put up at an inn with gables and leaded windows in a square lifted high above the roofs and triple cincture of the town wall'. There is only a single wall surrounding the town. Also it seems odd that Paddy did not record seeing the house where Vlad II Dracul lived in the 1430s which is next to that 'old clock over the archway'. Surely it would have been the obvious link to the story about Vlad Dracula that he goes on to recount since it was most likely his birthplace.

---

[4] Rothenburg ob der Tauber is a Bavarian town known for its well-preserved medieval buildings. In the Middle Ages, it was an Imperial Free City.

Although Paddy writes about the Lutheran Church on the Hill, he omits any mention of the 13th century Dominican cloister church opposite that 'old clock'. He slightly misses the point about Transylvanian church interiors since, before the introduction of Lutheranism, all interiors were decorated with wall paintings. It was the religious denomination that changed first. Hence the coffered and painted ceiling of the Calvinist Church in Mugeni and the frescoes in the Unitarian church in nearby Dârju are far from 'bleak and stripped'. Indeed, the frescoes on the walls of the Church on the Hill remained uncovered until the mid-18th century.

The references to Sándor Petőfi are strangely muted for here is the story of a poet of the 1848 Revolution. This is the young man who wrote:

> *Rise up, Magyar, the country calls!*
> *It's 'now or never' what fate befalls...*
> *Shall we live as slaves or free men?*
> *That's the question – choose your 'Amen'!*
> *God of Hungarians,*
> *we swear unto Thee,*
> *we swear unto Thee – that slaves we shall*
> *no longer be!*

Petőfi was killed fighting the Russians outside of Sighişoara on 31 July 1849. He was 26 years old.

One of the town's most famous features is the 300 steps that once connected the lower town to the *Bergschule* on the top of the hill. The last 175 steps known as the *Schülertreppe* were built in 1642 and are encapsulated in timber like a giant wooden caterpillar. Although he refers to it in his 1984 notebook, Paddy chooses to omit it.

Agnita/Szentágota/Agnetheln

On the way to Agnita, Paddy describes the architecture of the Saxon villages. He omits one defining feature of nearly all the houses – the year inscribed on or over an external beam which signifies the date they were last reconstructed.

The observation that 'at the heart of each village, sturdy churches reared squat, four-sided steeples with a tough, defensive look' is a generalisation. The peasant church at Bradeni/Henndorf which they passed has no such structure neither does the church at Saes/Schaas which has an 18th century polygonal spire, a feature shared by many village churches as a result of damage to the original structures by fire or earthquake.

The description of the church at Agnita is oddly inaccurate – 'a church as massive as a small bastille. Pierced by arrow-slits, the walls rose sheer, then expanded into machicolations and, above these, rows of short up-rights like squat pillars found galleries that hoisted pyramids of steeple'. Apart from losing its walls in the 19th century[5], the kirchenburg here is defined by a forbidding stand-alone fortified entrance tower, one of four that were once connected by a precinct wall. The church itself has an even higher [44m] fortified belfry tower at the West door with six levels and a gallery; the knave and choir are unfortified.

Paddy's assertion that 'massive church architecture was no defence against a determined enemy' is also incorrect. The watchtowers or 'turms' were manned during the hours of daylight and there was a well-practiced drill when the alarm was sounded; everyone knew what to do and supplies had already been stockpiled within the walls of the kirchenburg. What the marauders were usually after was people to sell in the slave markets of the Black Sea. Once the villagers were behind the walls, an enemy without artillery had no means of penetrating the defenses, which were covered by interlocking arcs of crossbow fire and later musket fire. In modern military parlance, the kirchenburgs were 'hard targets' which accounts for the fact that nearly all of them are still standing unscathed except for the depreda-tions of time. If Paddy had really been in the Burgenland, he would have grasped these facts.

And why did the loquacious wheelwright not tell the story of little Ursula who dressed in her devilish makeshift costume of leather cast-offs scared the raiders away with terrible howls? These teenage Saxon girls were a force to be reckoned: not far away at Hosman, young Lieschen drove the Tartars away by lobbing beehives at them!

Furthermore the 'roomy caves of the Carpathians' which Paddy tells us were where the villages drove their horses and cattle on the approach of raiders are hours away by foot from the most of the Saxon villages. This is a flight of fancy which surely would not have taken off if he had really made the 'secret journey'.

Fărgăraș/Forgaras/Fogarasch

Paddy's description of Cetatea Fărgăraș, one of the seats of the Transylvanian Diet and the residence of the wives of the Transylvanian Princes, is dis-tinctly odd: 'I had expected a daunting perpendicular stronghold, but apart from the donjon inside, it turned out to be a massive rectangle of ochre and brick-colour, almost a quarter of a mile square and slotted by embra-sures, with a circular bastion at each corner'.

---

[5] The materials were recycled in the construction of the pastor's house and school. This is typical of Saxon thrift.

The bastions are not circular but polygonal and Paddy makes no mention of the prominent ravelins at each corner of the rectangular plan which cover the defensive moat, the main element of the outer fortifications. Kurt Hielscher's 1933 photograph confirms that the broad almost lake-like moat was very much in evidence then as it is today.

While he attributes the final shape of the fortifications to Prince Gábor Bethlen, he entirely misses the point that it was Bethlen and then Prince Georgy Rákóczi I who, between them, created in the donjon one of the finest 17th century Renaissance residences in Transylvania with its elegant loggia overlooking the courtyard and Polish gothic casement windows.

Cârţa/Kerc/Kerz

This is the 'un-named' 13th century Cistercian abbey supposedly suppressed by Matthias on account of badly behaved monks. It includes both Gothic and Romanesque designs. Given the influence of the Cistercians in early Transylvania, it is strange that Paddy was not inspired by this dramatic ruin with its gaping wheel window now bereft of mullions and Gothic tracery that once must have housed a rose window. Surely this would have prompted him to enquire further into how these frontier monks arrived so far to the East of their Burgundian heartland.

The story of how this order spread with such fervent velocity to the distant borderlands of Hungary from the Abbey at Clairvaux in the 12th and 13th centuries is surely one of the wonders of the Middle Ages. Cistercians first appeared in Hungary in 1179 when Agnes de Châtillon, the first wife of King Béla III [1172–96], founded a monastery at Igris/Egres, now in Timiş county Romania. Béla's son, King Endre II [1205–35] and his second wife, Yolanda de Courtenay, the daughter of the hapless Byzantine Emperor Peter II, lie buried there. Another Cistercian abbey at Pilis outside Budapest, founded by Béla in 1184, became the burial place of Gertrude de Merania, King Endre II's first wife who was murdered while out hunting by Hungarian nobles incensed by her pro-German stance. This is the very stuff of early Hungarian history.

Sibiu/ Szeben/ Hermannstadt

Did the gallivanting trio not notice Baron Bruckenthal's imposing 18th century Baroque summer residence on the main road at Avrig, albeit a sanatorium at the time? Its formal gardens, modelled in miniature on those at Schönbrunn and Laxenburg, descend in layers of terraces down to the river and dissolve into the first English park planted in Romania in 1778.

Time and space become confused for Selimbar/Sellenberk is on the outskirts of Sibiu/Szeben.

The party drove 'across market places and great flagged squares'. There is only one great market place in Sibiu which was entirely cobbled in 1934 and compares favourably to the great marktplätze of Lübeck and Halle. Overlooking it is Sacheverell Sitwell's 'chief curiosity [of Sibiu]', the imposing late Baroque Palace of Baron Bruckenthal, Maria-Theresa's governor of Transylvania. Why did Elemér not include in his list of artists the Van Dyck painting of King Charles 1 and Queen Henrietta in the Bruckenthal Palace, albeit a copy?

Sebeş/Szászsebes/Mühlbach

No mention of the superb gothic carvings of saints sheltering under stone canopies on the exterior of the church at Sebeş/Szászsebes on the way back to Déva.

Other oddities

Given that 'the roads were not good: the car pitched about the ruts and potholes like a boat on a choppy sea', the journey time from Sighişoara to Deva via Fărgăraş and Sibiu is nothing short of miraculous.

Another fly in the story ointment is the identity and motivation of 'Angela'. Paddy makes it clear that she was Xenia Csernovics. What did her mother and sisters make of her sudden absence? Would she really have felt her reputation would be safe in Cluj and Târgu Mures, the two busiest Hungarian towns in the whole of Transylvania? Given that she was related on her father's side to the Bethlens, Ghykas and Kinskys, her amorous escapade would have been foolhardy to say the least. Furthermore, the Beteghs, her husband's family, came from Turda and were related to the count Horváth de Széplak family.

With its uncharacteristic paucity of observation and lack of enquiry together with many inexplicable omissions and indeed baffling inaccuracies, Paddy's patchy testimony of his Transylvania circuit is worrisome.

The answer to these inconsistencies and omissions was later revealed in a letter[6] Paddy wrote to Rudi Fischer, a Hungarian academic who was writing for *The Hungarian Quarterly* and had previously flagged up his concerns about accuracy. He confessed that, 'bar Zam and Gurasada and a bit further in', he had not been to Transylvania other than a short trip to Fărgăraş 'which I failed to take in properly' and to Hermannstadt [Sibiu] which he had made when staying with Count Antoniu Mocsonyi, the

---

[6] NLS Acc.13338/44–45 Letter PLF to Rudi Fischer 22 November 1984.

Marshal of the Royal Court, in Sinaia during his time in Bucharest in the autumn of 1934.

It was only when he visited Transylvania in 1984 [a previous trip planned for 1982 had been cancelled] that he saw 'Alba Julia, Torda, Kolosvar, M.Vasarhely, above all Segesvar and the Saxon villages and churches'[7]. The Hotel New York in Cluj had become the Hotel Continental, 'hence the wealth of detail about the décor'. He went on to explain how 'the highly improper idea occurred to me of planting my 1984 Transylvania into the 1934 'Triple Fugue' [chapter], as a means of recapturing my latter day journey'. He confided in Fischer 'well, here's my guilty secret which you are the only other living soul to share'.

Rudi Fischer told Artemis Cooper in 2012 that 'the whole drive through Transylvania was invented…what is more, inspired by and based on a book I had given him'.[8]

Paddy, as a former SOE operative, kept true to his literary cover story and repeated his fabrication in the *Daily Telegraph* article of 12 May 1990, 'weeks strewn with strange adventures which ended in a rackety midsummer jaunt with a wild and enterprising girl re-named Angéla, all over Transylvania. In a vast borrowed car, the three of us explored the old cities of Alba Julia and Cluj and the important Magyar town of Tîrgu Mures, the centre of the land of the Székelys, who had settled there in the tenth century. Careering on, we struck south to Sighişoara, the castellated and tapering stronghold of Vlad the Impaler. Next day we all parted, and, very sadly, I was on my own again'.

The reference to Sighişoara as the stronghold of Vlad the Impaler is an invention; Vlad may or may not have been born in Sighisoara before he was sent as a hostage to Egrigoz in Anatolia in bond to the Sultan for his father's 'good behaviour'. Like his father, Vlad made the castle of Târgovişte in the foothills of the southern Carpathians his capital. So it is somewhat ironic that Paddy takes a swipe at Bram Stoker's *Dracula*. 'The fact that Transylvania is a region of castles, forests, counts and vampires, and that some confused strands of local history have managed to tangle themselves into the novel's local colour, has always [for me] set it beyond charm's reach'.

To be sure, Stoker's Count Dracula is an altogether different figure from Vlad Dracul II, the figment of an Irish actor-manager's fertile imagination in 1897. Probably influenced by fellow Irish writer, J. Sheridan Le

---

[7] Here he typically uses redundant Hungarian place names. In Romanian, the list reads Alba Julia, Turda, Cluj Napoca, Târgu Mureş and Sighişoara.

[8] Artemis Cooper: *Paddy Leigh Fermour, An Adventure*.

Fanu's novella, "*Carmilla*", a story set in Styria where "the sun sets with all its melancholy splendour behind the sylvan horizon", and the Hungarian traveller Ármin Vámbéry, Stoker picks up a Wallachian warlord, moves him a hundred and fifty miles north, converts him into a Székely and with a final flourish of the pen invests him with the attributes of a vampire.

When it comes to fictitious Transylvanian landscapes, writing in his house in St Leonard's Terrace just off the King's Road in Chelsea, Stoker gives Paddy a run for his money. Jonathan Harker, the hapless solicitor from Surrey, arrives in Bistrița from Cluj and then heads for Borgo Prund in Bucovina via the Borgo pass. So far so good: these places do exist in north east Transylvania. After a dramatic rendezvous somewhere in the Carpathians, Harper is conscious of his driver pulling up "in a courtyard of a vast ruined castle, from whose tall black windows came no ray of light, and whose broken battlements showed a jagged line against the moonlight sky". Later he notes that "the castle is on the very edge of a terrible precipice. A stone falling from the window would fall a thousand feet without touching anything! As far as the eye can reach is a sea of green tree-tops, with occasionally a deep rift where there is a chasm. Here and there are silver threads where the rivers wind in deep gorges through the forests"

When John Hillaby in his *Journey Through Europe* [1972] found himself on the trail of Hilaire Belloc as he crossed the Vosges mountains, he wondered how on earth Belloc had managed to get through in a straight line. He found the answer in *The Path to Rome*: 'for though it is permissible, and a pleasant thing [as Bacon says], to mix a little falsehood with one's truth…yet is it much more delectable, and far worthier of the immortal spirit of man to soar into the empyrean of pure lying – that is, to lay the bridle on the neck of Pegasus and let him go forward, while in the saddle meanwhile one sits well back, grips with the knee, takes the race, and on the energy of that steed visits the wheeling stars.' Surely Paddy would not have demurred.

1922 Coronation

János Hunyadi

Alba Iulia

Turda salt 1934

Salt miners 1900

Bánffy Palace in Cluj 1930s

Hotel New York in Cluj 1930s

The Ascension of the Lord Orthodox Cathedral in Târgu Mures 1930s

The Town Hall and Palace of Culture in Târgu Mures 1930s

Sighişoara 1933

The old clock tower Sighişoara 2017

The kirchenburg at Agnita

The Cetatea at Făgăraș 1933

The Cistercian monastery at Cârța

Baron Bruckenthal's summer residence at Avrig

Market place in Sibiu 1933

Baron Bruckenthal's Palace in Sibiu 1930s

Chapter Four

BUCHAREST

23 October –14 November 1934

'It was…a time of entertaining and parties and tremendous luncheons and dinners…'

~ *The Broken Road*

Twenty-seven years after *Between the Woods and the Water* was published, a posthumous Paddy, through the medium of his diaries and with the help of his literary executors, recounts in *The Broken Road* [2013] how he interrupted his travels through Bulgaria to return to Romania in the late autumn of 1934 to stay with friends in Bucharest. Crossing the Danube at Rustchuk – a strange Turkish term he chose to use for Ruse – he set off for Bucharest in a monotonous straight line, passing peasants, herdsmen and gypsies going about their everyday business in the vast unrelenting flatness of the Wallachian plain, an experience which brushed him with melancholia and sadness. An overnight stop with a Jewish grocer results in one of the great lines of the book: 'It's easy to be a good Jew, impossible to be a good Christian.'

In Giurgiu, a small town on the Danube, Paddy wrote two letters in search of a bed. Although not identified by name, Count Antoniu Mocsonyi was one of the recipients. The other letter was directed to Count Ambrose O'Kelly de Gallagh [1888–1970] and his wife, Elena née Filipescu, who later had Paddy to stay for the weekend in their house in Sinaia. Like many a young Irish gentleman in the 18th century, one of Count Ambrose's ancestors, Dillon O'Kelly, had left Ireland in search of fame and fortune in warring Europe. After joining the Austrian army, he married Marian, Countess of Klenowa, a favourite of the Empress Maria Theresa and widow of the Hereditary Treasurer of Bohemia. In recognition of what was described as 'the great antiquity and celebrity' of the O'Kelly family and 'having also favourably considered the faithful and praiseworthy military services that have been rendered by Dillon O'Kelly during the last eleven years and which are still being rendered by him in the capacity as Captain', in November 1767 the Empress granted the O'Kellys 'the Imperial and Royal grace of being raised, he and all his legitimate descendants and their heirs, whether male or female, to the rank and dignity of Counts and Countesses of our Kingdom, Principality and Hereditary States', and in addition granted to them the title of *Hochwohlgeboren*. Although Dillon O'Kelly was childless, by virtue of the grant being issued to his father Festus in Ireland, the title of Count remained within the immediate family.

During the summer and autumn of 1934, Bucharest was in the midst of massive modernization. Its population had increased from 350,000 at the beginning of the decade to 800,000 and the city, with a modicum of justification, claimed to be the Paris of the Balkans. Certainly, no other Balkan city could offer the glamorous cafes and luxury shops that lined the Calea Victoriei. Yet political stability remained elusive after the assassination of Prime Minister Duca the previous December and the Iron Guard continued to flourish. In the middle of Paddy's stay, on 9 October King Carol's brother-in-law King Alexander of Yugoslavia was shot dead in Marseilles at the start of a state visit to France. The killing by a Bulgarian IMRO gunman hired by the Croatian revolutionary Ustaša movement was captured on film and the sight of Alexander lying dead in his finery in the back of his official car prompted Carol to cancel his own birthday celebrations scheduled for 15 October. After attending the funeral in Belgrade, he only reappeared in Bucharest at the end of November. These were dangerous times for Balkan monarchs and their ministers.

Once in Bucharest and ensconced in the Savoy-Ritz with Madame Tania from Bessarabia and her collection of five young female 'lodgers' who conveniently represent the regions of Romania – one from the Bucovina, another from the Dobrudja, then a Moldavian, a Transylvanian and a Saxon. How close to paradise Paddy must have been as he immersed himself in city life. Or did he? Bucharest in 1934 was booming for oil revenues ensured the city never slept. Music, art, architecture and sculpture were all freeing themselves from the imitative French relationship: there was now a vibrant Romanian creative zeitgeist and national identity. Yet nowhere does he comment on what was going on around him. On the contrary, through his adulation of and association with the Phanariot grandees and his stay with Josias von Rantzau zu Panker und Tralauf, Paddy is destined to look back, possessed by a nostalgia for their world which he himself will never know. His expedition to Sinaia in a chauffeur driven limousine is contaminated with a melancholic sense of entrapment – 'I felt as torpid as an autumn fly, weighed down with depression'. On reaching Brasov he bemoans 'how I wished…that I had arrived on foot [and] dumped my kit…' In all of this simmers a precarious tension between the joie de vie of a carefree scholar gypsy and the vicarious pleasure of a precocious socialite mixing with grandees.

Among the glitterati of Bucharest with whom he rubs shoulders, Paddy mentions Marcelle Catargiu, descendant of Barbu Catargiu [1807–62], the first Prime Minister of Romania and the first of five[1] to be assassinated; Angy Dancos[2], of whom, apart from being 'a sweet Rumanian type' and married, little is known; the 22-year-old 'aviator' Prince Constantin Soutzo [1912–2004], who had recently married Princess Roxana Callimachi [1918–78], the 16-year-old daughter of Prince Ioan and Princess Anne-Marie Callimachi[3]; the Oxford-educated 25-year-old banker and Queen Marie's godson, Nicky Chrissoveloni [1909–1972] whose great-grandfather had escaped the clutches of the Turks in the horrific 1822 massacre in Chios[4]; and the diplomat, Michael Palairet [1882–1956], who as British Minister Plenipotentiary to Romania had been instrumental in mending the fences with King Carol II after his expulsion from Britain in 1928.

In *The Broken Road*, Paddy adds more names 'flitting about the middle distance' – Nicolae Titulescu, Grigore and Nouchette Gafencu, Prince Antoine and Elizabeth Bibesco and their daughter Priscilla [14-years-old at the time], Princess Maruca Cantacuzene, Rose Covarrubias Nano,

---

[1] Catargiu, Duca, Călinescu, Iorga and Argeşanu.

[2] Danco is a surname in Bucharest.

[3] The marriage lasted two years; Roxana never remarried. Constantin later emigrated to Canada and became a cattle rancher in Calgary.

[4] Arrested and imprisoned by the Communists in 1948, Nicky was allowed to immigrate to Greece in 1960.

Paul Zanesco and Hélène Yourievitch, Prince Georghe and Elizabeth Cantacuzene, Prince Dimitri Sturdza, Gregoire Duca, Perico and Lili Prat, and Princess Julie Ghika[5]. He asks himself whether he could or should add to it and although he would like it to continue 'a great deal longer', he decides that it is best to stick to the rule 'either out [of Rumania] or dead'. In his list, six are 'out' and nine are dead. The ones needed to complete the list were either missing or existing in 'great distress and poverty' in the Communist regime.

In her literary study *Inventing Ruritania*, Vesna Goldsworthy groups together the two guests at Princess Callimachi's lunch party in 1936 in their mutual tristesse. 'Sacheverell Sitwell and, to some degree, Patrick Leigh Fermor lament the passing of a feudal world, the Europe of peasants and princes … Their melancholy reminiscences about the decaying palaces in the East, the pre-industrial Arcadias of Europe's Orient, with their Romanticist, more or less openly anti-urban and anti-modernist agenda, are [again] unmistakably British.'

---

[5] Née von Reineck; married to Dumitru Ghika.

PART 2
1935–1945

'…and as the wind howled around us and the harness of the horses jangled in front, it seemed as if we were in an old Russian novel.'

~Derek Patmore, *Invitation to Romania*

Give to me the life I love
Let the lave go by me,
Give the jolly heaven above
And the byway night me.
Bed in the bush with stars to see,
Bread I dip in the river –
There's the life for a man like me,
There's the life for ever.

~Robert Louis Stevenson: *The Vagrant, Songs of Travel*

DESCRIPTIO MOLDAVIAE

'In those days Rumania sounded remote, and Moldavia…remoter still'.

~ *Words of Mercury*

Paddy returned to Romania in May 1935, this time to the former Principality of Moldavia which marched with Bessarabia to the East and South and the Bucovina to the North. Transylvania lay to the West behind a wall of *massifs* and wild forests that straddle the Eastern Carpathian Mountains. It was an entirely different world from the Banat and Transylvania with their German and Hungarian antecedents. This was the real Romania, the borderland with the Eurasian steppes where for centuries a ceaseless and relentless power struggle between avaricious Empires raged. A world once of fur-coated boyars with quaint feudal titles – Voievod [the ruler], Logofăt [chancellor], Vistier [treasurer] Paharnic [cup bearer], Postelnic [chamberlain], Hatman [general], Stolnic [steward], Vornic [chief justice] – before they became Dragomans and donned Turkish kalpaks and richly embroidered caftans in deference to their Ottoman suzerains, the Moldavians had only been universally adopted Western dress and etiquette a mere ninety years before Paddy's first visit.

Such are the multitude of differences between Moldavian history and those of Transylvania and the Banat that the former Principality merits its own short chapter for it was here that Paddy was to spend on and off five of his most formative years.

After the Hungarians had first conquered Transylvania, they recruited settlers from the lower Rhine to populate it and defend the passes in the Eastern Carpathian Mountains. Beyond this natural barrier lay the open spaces of the steppe from where the Mongols launched their murderous invasion in 1241, nearly destroying the entire Hungarian kingdom. Providence intervened when news of the death of Ogedei reached his armies in Europe; his generals returned to elect a new Khan. As a result, the Hungarian Kings were able to use the vacuum and consolidate their grip on their eastern frontier by enforcing the power and influence of the crown. For the Voivode Bogdan of Maramureş, who had defiantly refused the title of *comes* and its terms of deference to the King, this represented an opportunity and he crossed the Carpathians and settled in *Terra Moldovana,* called after the river Moldau which flowed through it.

Wasting little time, Bogdan adopted the ox head or auroch and a star as his coat of arms and minted his own coinage in neighbouring Poland. Soon markets sprung up and in 1374 the Patriarch of Ochrid[1] consecrated the first bishopric in Suceava. Taking a leaf out of the Hungarian book of governance, the Prince, known as Hospodar from the Slavonic *Gospodar* or Lord, assumed absolute powers over his boyars or nobles. His council was purely advisory.

Borders in those days were somewhat ill-defined since the Prince did not have the resources to police and defend them but a rough estimate shows the eastern boundary of Moldavia following the Dniester river (now running through western Ukraine), the southern one from just West of Odessa to Buzau, the western one from the Carpathians north to Chernivtsi (now in Ukraine) and then back across to the Dniester river. Today, within these boundaries, lie the Romanian province of Moldavia, the independent state of Moldova, and the Ukrainian lands along the Danube including Bilhorod and, in the north, Procutia[2].

The problem that came to dominate Moldavian politics for the next four

---

[1] A Hellenised see in Macedonia.

[2] The area of the Ukraine on the North and North-east of Moldavia. Formerly a province of Poland.

hundred years was Turkey. Nineteen years before Bogdan first crossed the mountains, Bulgaria had come under attack from the Ottomans. In 1371 the regional power of Greater Serbia went into decline after the battle of Marica River, a disaster compounded by the victory of Sultan Murad 1 at Kosovo eighteen years later. Ominously Sultan Bayezid invaded Wallachia, Moldavia's southern neighbour, in 1391. Attempts by the Hungarians to alleviate the situation came to nothing when a crusade led by King Sigismund was crushingly defeated at Nicopolis in 1396. Ironically, it was another Mongol advance in the East that saved the day: in 1402, Amir Timur captured the Sultan Bayezid and the acquisitive Ottoman war machine temporarily went into abeyance.

In 1417, Wallachia, the principality on Moldavia's southern border, started to pay an annual tribute of 3,000 ducats to 'the Porte' as the Ottoman government was styled by Western states but it was Hungary that the Turks really wanted. Sultan Murad invaded Transylvania and was only stopped by the military genius of one man, János Hunyadi, a Wallachian by birth and the only person claimed today by both the Hungarians and Romanians[3] as a national hero. This brilliant soldier checked the Turks at Belgrade in 1441, defeated them at Alba Julia the next year and the following year scored a resounding victory at Nis that led to a ten-year peace treaty.

Another towering figure emerged at this point, this time a young Turk, Sultan Mehmet II. After capturing Constantinople in 1453, he pushed west to Belgrade when Hunyadi confronted him. It was a sad day in August 1456, when this 'Athlete of Christ' died of the plague, leaving his son, Matthias Corvinus, in charge. Now it was the turn of Moldavia to produce an outstanding leader, Stephen the Great or *Stefan cel Mare*.

It is hard to describe the awe and reverence that Stefan is still held in Romania today[4]; the English equivalent of Stefan merges the legendary exploits of Elizabeth I, Essex, Cecil, Raleigh and Drake and a dollop of Churchillian obstinacy into one person, producing a national hero of massive stature. He was by the standard of his time – and many would venture of any time – a character genuinely worthy of the extravagant accolades bestowed on him by history.

1457 was an unpropitious year to become Prince of Moldavia for, after the fall of Constantinople, Eastern Europe stood nakedly exposed to the new Ottoman super power. Stefan could not rely on Hungary, for Matthias

---

[3] Known to the Romanians as Ion Hunyadi or Huniade; also referred to as John Corvinus and as Johann Corvin von Hunniad, Prince of Siebenburgen.

[4] In 2006, the public voted Stefan the 'greatest Romanian of all time' in a *Televiziurea Română* poll.

was looking West towards Bohemia and Austria for new conquests; he could not rely on Casimir of Poland, who was embroiled in the Baltic and Lithuania; nor could he rely on Ivan of Moscow, who faced the ever persistent Tatar threat. The obvious solution for this new 22-year-old ruler was to pay a tribute to the Porte and enjoy a quiet life. This was not to be the way of Stefan.

First, he set about organising an army of 50,000 men, recruited from all over Moldavia; equipped only with padded jackets and home-made weapons, this was no hi-tech force but it could mobilise and disperse in a week. Then he created a series of massive stone fortresses, either reconstructed or built anew: all were capable of withstanding artillery fire and long sieges. In 1465, he captured the Danube fort of Chilia, an action that provoked King Matthias of Hungary, who wanted his Eastern neighbour to be weak, to attack him in November 1467. Stefan shrewdly withdrew his forces from the line of advance and lured Matthias to Baia where on 14 December, in a daring night attack, he cut the Hungarian army to pieces. Moldavia was never again troubled by Hungary.

Meanwhile, the Ottomans had completed the conquest of Serbia and Bosnia and in 1470 were poised for an all-out attack on Hungary. Radu the Handsome, the new Prince of Wallachia, was in no way minded to stop them. Stefan, knowing that Moldavia was also on the Ottoman shopping list, acted decisively. In 1473 he replaced Radu with his own nominee and waited. This infuriated the Sultan Mehmet II who sent Stefan a note to the effect that he was to surrender the Black Sea fortress of Chilia immediately and pay an annual tribute to the Porte. Stefan refused.

So, in the summer of 1474, a powerful Ottoman army under the Grand Vizir Suleiman the Eunuch, together with Besarab of Wallachia (the very man Stefan had replaced Radu with) attacked Moldavia. Once more, Stefan showed himself a master of strategy; he withdrew the population northwards, denying all supplies to the enemy and rendering roads impassable. On 10 January 1475, Stefan attacked the Ottomans at Vaslui and inflicted a crushing defeat on them – four high-ranking pashas were killed and 100 flags captured. As the historian, Hugh Seton Watson, wrote: 'So, the country that was modestly set up, little over a century before, at the foot of the Eastern Carpathians, got an unexpected international status.'[5]

Stefan now turned to the West for help in 'cutting off the pagan's right hand'. He wrote: '*I have pursued the enemies of Christendom, I defeated them, crushed them down and by our sword they perished.*' He warned that the Sultan would soon come '*with all his might against us to subjugate Moldavia, the gate*

---

[5] *A History of the Roumanians.*

of the Christian world that God so far has protected. If this gate, which is our country, is lost – God forbid! –then the entire Christian world will be in great peril.' Pope Sixtus IV, genuinely moved by this appeal, addressed Stefan as *athleta Christi*[6], a title previously bestowed on Janos Hunyadi when he raised the siege of Belgrade. But they were empty words for no help came.

Mehmet, incensed by the defeat at Vaslui, personally took charge of a new invasion in 1476. With his Northern flank threatened by the Tartars who were in league with the Ottomans, Stefan found himself overstretched and was defeated at Răsboeini in July. He fled to Poland but with cholera in its ranks and no supplies to live on, the Ottoman Army was forced to fall back and with the timely arrival of a friendly Hungarian army, Stefan returned post-haste from Poland and was able to harass the Turks back across the Danube. Mehmet considerably left Stefan alone after this.

On Mehmet's death in 1481, Stefan once again went into Wallachia and took control of it in order to create a buffer zone against the Turks. In 1484, the new Sultan, Bayezid II, seized Chilia and Cetatea Alba, the two great fortresses and trading posts which both protected Stefan's Danube flank and contributed handsomely to his exchequer. This was a blow for what had once been dubbed the Tartar road, the trade route which linked Poland to the Black Sea, had become a prosperous Moldavian commercial artery and these two fortresses its critical transport terminals. A year later, the Turks plundered and burnt Suceava although Stefan, with the help of Casimir of Poland, defeated them at Cătlăbuga as they retired south. It was more of the same in 1486 with Stefan once more prevailing, this time at Scheia to the North of Roman.

The rest of his reign was a constant tussle with the Porte, not helped by the intrigues of Poland and Hungary muddying the political waters. A Polish-Turkish peace was concluded in 1489, leaving Stefan with little choice other than to open peace negotiations himself and to finally pay tribute to the Porte. A last attempt in 1500–1502 was made to retake Cetatea Alba and Chilia – the loss of the latter had always stuck in Stefan's throat since he had employed over 800 masons and 17,000 labourers to build it in 1479 – but it came to nought. Two years before his death in 1504, Stefan told the Venetian envoy: 'I am surrounded on all sides by enemies and have fought thirty-six battles since I was lord of this country, of these won thirty-four and lost two.' He was indeed a true champion of 16th century Christendom.

The Romanian historian, Miron Costin, summed Stefan up with per-spicacity: 'acute of judgment, sober, not proud, but a stubborn defender of

---

[6] 'Verus Christianae fidei athleta'

his rights, in war always on the spot, well versed in military science, generally favoured by victory, never depressed by misfortune: ever expecting a better turn to affairs. The Moldavians think of him in political respects, with that veneration with which one holds a saint in religious honour'. On 21 June 1992, the Romanian church sanctified Stefan; magnanimously, his sword pilfered by the Turks in 1538, was loaned by the Topkapi Museum in Istanbul for the occasion.

Stefan's heirs struggled to maintain Moldavia's independence. His son, Bogdan the One Eyed, succeeded him and almost immediately had to do a deal with the Porte. In return for complete autonomy, respect for Christianity, non-interference with Princely elections, and an undertaking that no mosques were built and no Turkish land ownership permitted, Bogdan parted with 4,000 ducats, forty broodmares and forty falcons per annum. Alas such treaties were more honoured in breach than observance and Bogdan was killed fighting the Tartar allies of the Ottomans in 1517.

Turkish eyes as always were still on Hungary and on 26 August 1526, Sultan Suleiman comprehensively defeated King Lajos at Mohács; the dead included the young King, five bishops, many nobles and around 50,000 soldiers, most of whom were mercenaries. Soon after, in 1527, Petru Rares, an illegitimate son of Stefan, was elected to the Moldavian throne. Petru's career was characterised by intrigue on a Byzantine scale which meant war with the Porte was inevitable, In 1538, the Ottomans over-ran Moldavia and Petru found himself spending a year in a Transylvanian prison. When his gaoler, Zápolyai, died in 1540, with a mesmerising mixture of abject pleading, mouth-watering presents and non-stop flattery, Petru succeeded in persuading the Sultan to reinstall him. He returned triumphant but poorer for the new terms were onerous: a standing bodyguard of 500 muscle-bound Ottomans, tribute raised from 4,000 to 12,000 ducats per annum and his son to be held hostage in Constantinople.

The wily Petru died in 1546, by now an irrelevance to the Porte after the fall of Buda in 1541. His son, Ilias, the hostage, had by then become a Muslim and after a few years on the Moldavian throne decided that the job offer of Pasha of Silistria was more conducive to his ambitions, so he was succeeded by his younger son, Stefan, who died of debauchery after a reign of only eighteen months. In 1592, Alexander the Bad, the last descendant of Stefan, was hanged in public in Istanbul. Stefan's dynasty had disappeared in less than a hundred years on account of its own ineptitude and the political efficacy of its enemies. The 19th century traveller Anatole de Demidoff summarized that 'from this date commenced, for both principalities, an era of indolence, uncertainty and discouragement. Although the voivodes continued to be named by the boyars with a vain form of election, it was in reality by the Divan of Constantinople that these princes, the obedient vassals of the Porte, were chosen, and frequently, at its caprice, deprived of power and life'.

After several attempts to throw off Ottoman suzerainty, the second half of the 17th century was marked by vainglorious attempts by the boyars to establish their own regime in Moldavia. These all failed, and it was only when Ottoman power was in decline at the end of the century that a glimmer of light appeared on the western horizon. After the great military achievements of the Köprülü Grand Viziers, the Porte suffered a dramatic change in fortune when Kara Mustafa Köprülü failed to seize Vienna and the Ottoman army was roundly defeated at the battle of Karlenburg by a coalition of Imperial Austrian and Polish armies in 1683. This failure, under the very walls of the imperial capital, spelt the beginning of the withdrawal of Ottoman forces from the middle Danube region, a retreat marked by a series of defeats that forced the Porte to conclude the treaty of Karlowitz in 1699.

This great counter-attack found the three Romanian lands in markedly different situations. Transylvania, which had become the front line of the Imperial *reconquista*, was annexed by Vienna and subjected to such vigorous Catholic proselytising and harsh taxation that a rebellion inevitably followed. The Prince of Moldavia, Michael Racovitza, confronted by a significant economic and demographic decline, thought about turning to Russia with whom his subjects shared a common faith and thus made an infinitely more preferable ally than the Habsburg emperor with his counter-reformation agenda. Distance was of course a handicap, but the victory of Peter the Great over King Charles X of Sweden at Poltava in 1709, had enhanced the prestige of Russia. His boyars feared than such a defection would trigger the imposition of an Ottoman *eyalit* – direct rule from Istanbul – and ousted him. The Porte quickly appointed Nicholas Mavrocordatos as Prince. A Greek originally from a family in Chios, he did not speak a word of Romanian and introduced Greek manners, Greek language and Greek costumes in a court noted for its sophistication.

The election of Dimitrie Cantemir marked the zenith of Moldavian-born Princes. This extraordinary gifted prince and scholar was born in 1673, second son of a successful soldier, Constatin Cantemir, Prince of Moldavia from 1685 to 1693. According to family legend, the founder of the family was a Tartar, Khan Temir[7], who had settled in Moldavia in the sixteenth century. The name had become elided to Cantemir. Educated

---

[7] Better known in English as Tamerlane the Great or Christopher Marlow's Tamburlaine.

first at Iaşi in the Classics and Slavonic languages, Dimitrie demonstrated an astonishing memory and when he was sent to Istanbul in 1688 in bond for his father's good behaviour as Prince, he enrolled at the Academy of the Orthodox Patriarchy and soon gained access to its great treasury of Islamic learning, becoming fluent in Turkish, Arabic, Persian and Tartar.

The young Prince also became an accomplished *tanbur*[8] player and a popular figure at the Imperial court at Topkapi Sarayi where he presented the Sultan with *The Book of the Science of Music through Letters*, a study dealing with the melodic and rhythmic structure and practice of Ottoman music including 350 scores. His residence in Ortaky, which he had bought in 1693 from the Sultan's brother-in-law, became a centre of intellectual and political debate, attracting philosophers, rhetoricians, annotators of the Koran, musicians, painters, miniaturists, mathematicians and translators.

In March 1693 Dimitrie was elected Prince of Moldavia by the boyars on the death of his father but by April he had failed to come up with the money demanded by the Ottomans and had to stand down in favour of another candidate, Constantin Duca, who had been bankrolled by the Prince of Wallachia, Constantin Brâncoveanu. Dimitrie returned to Istanbul; his older brother, Antioh, was subsequently appointed ruler in 1695.

In 1699, the year of Dimitrie's marriage to Cassandra Cantacuzino, the daughter of Serban Cantacuzino the former ruler of Wallachia, the Peace of Karlowitz between Vienna and the Porte changed the Moldavian political landscape forever. The Habsburgs recovered all of Hungary except the Banat, all of Croatia-Slavonia and the whole of Transylvania. Poland consented to withdraw from Moldavia, which it had been occupying on and off for the last decade, and the Porte abandoned its claims to the Ukraine (Russia took a further two years to reach agreement with the Sultan: Azov was ceded to Moscow in 1702). These dramatic changes heralded that Turkey was now perceived as a power in decline.

For Moldavia, the new reality equated to living next door to two new superpowers, the Habsburg Empire and the up-and-coming Russian one, while at the same time being beholden to the Porte. When he finally succeeded to the Moldavian throne in 1710, Dimitrie had long ago come to the conclusion that a war between these regional superpowers was inevitable; furthermore, Moldavia would be right in the middle of it. In November that year, the Ottomans predictably declared war on Russia, so Dimitrie did a deal with Peter the Great; in return for Moldavian support

---

[8] An Iranian guitar-like instrument. Its derivatives include the Greek buzuki and the Indian sitar.

for Russia, Cantemir secured the hereditary title of Prince and, as an insurance policy, a pension and estates in Russia if it all went wrong. And that indeed was just what happened.

Peter who had recklessly advanced way ahead of the main body of his army, found himself and his advance guard of 38,000 facing a well-equipped 135,000 strong Turkish army at Stănileşti on the River Prut in July 1711. A 50,000 force of bloodthirsty Crimea Tartars swam across the river to engage the Russians whilst the main Ottoman body of troops secured the bridges and outflanked Peter.

Surrounded and short of supplies, Peter proposed terms which were readily agreed to – Azov was handed back, a large bribe was paid to the Grand Vizier and Russian interference in the affairs of Poland renounced. Dimitrie, now horribly exposed to the Porte for his duplicity, had no choice but to flee. He managed to escape the clutches of the Turks by swathing himself in rugs in the Empress Catherine's barouche as she headed back to Moscow and thus began life as an exile in Russia. He was lucky for his opposite number in Wallachia, Prince Constantin Brâncoveanu, who had done a similar deal but with the Habsburgs rather than the Tsar, was summoned with his family to Istanbul in 1714 and summarily beheaded with his two sons and son-in-law.

Dimitrie's wife Cassandra died in 1713, leaving him with six children[9] under the age of fourteen. Now aged forty-four, he married Anastasia Trubecka, a seventeen-year-old Russian princess the same age as his eldest daughter Maria[10]. He lived the rest of his life at Harcov near Moscow and died on his estate at Dimitrievska in 1723. This extraordinary man, famed throughout Europe for his erudition, left as his legacy three great histories, all written while in exile in Russia. *Descriptio Moldaviae*, written between 1714 and 1716 and printed in Latin, German and Russian, was an extensive survey on the history and culture of Moldavia with a fine map attached, drawn by the Prince himself. His second Romanian history was entitled *A Chronicle of the Entire Romanian Land* and was written in Romanian between 1719 and 1722. Here for the first time was advanced the spurious claim that all the inhabitants of Romania – Moldavians, Transylvanians and Wallachians – were the descendants of Trajan's colonists and had pure undiluted Roman blood. Nothing was left of the Dacian gene.

But his greatest history was *Incrementa et decrementa Aulae Othmannicae* or *Growth and Decay of the Ottoman Empire*, a history of the Ottoman empire published in Latin, English, French and German. His knowledge of

---

[9] His son became the Russian ambassador to France and a talented playwright.

[10] She later became the mistress of Peter the Great.

this subject was so encyclopaedic that the 579 pages of text were supported by 485 pages of notes! A second sister volume, 'System of the Mohammedan Religion' offered a commentary about the faiths, cultures and education of the Arab, Turkish and Persian peoples, taking a sympathetic view of the moral and artistic facets of the Islamic world.

To replace Cantemir, the Porte sent a previous Phanariot Prince, Nicholas Mavrocordatos, to Iaşi, this time to ensure the support of the boyars. His reappointment marked the beginning of what came to be known as the Phanariot century [1712 – 1821], best described as one of enlightened absolutism but not in a strictly pejorative sense for Moldavian society was gradually modernised. It coincided with an intensification of Habsburg and Russian ploys to divide up the territories of the ailing Ottoman Empire. The Romanian lands, especially Moldavia, were the main stage in this struggle between these two great powers. Through the treaty of Passarowitz in 1718 which ended the Austrian-Ottoman war, the Habsburg empire annexed the Banat and Oltenia. During the Russian-Ottoman war [1776–1774], the Porte ceded Bucovina and northern Moldavia to the Hapsburgs, and through the treaty of Bucharest in 1812, which ended the Russian-Ottoman war [1806–1812], Russia annexed the territory of Moldavia between the Prut and Dniester rivers, which came to be known as Bessarabia, a name previously applied only to the extreme southern part of this territory that had once been under the rule of the Bessarab princes of Wallachia. The Moldavia of Stefan the Great had been ineluctably reduced.

A bungled anti-Phanariot uprising in Wallachia in 1821 coincided with the Greek War of Independence against Ottoman rule. In the light of what he considered the massive treason of the Greeks, the Sultan decided to remove the Phanariots and their Greek functionaries and reinstall the native princes. He also returned control of the hugely valuable monasteries to the two princes of Wallachia and Moldavia. Once again, due to external circumstances, the political structure of the principalities had been reconfigured, this time for the better.

In early March 1848, news of the revolutions in Europe reached Moldavia. Posters appeared in Iaşi, criticising the ruling Prince Michael Sturdza and calling for reform. Sturdza responded in late March by publishing a Russian despatch that declared the Tsar's active opposition to 'any further spread of the anarchy and deterioration of the ties between the two principalities and the Porte'. Caught between a possible Tsarist intervention and a potential revolution, Sturdza secured the support of the garrison in Iaşi, and then responded decisively. He arrested and exiled the main leaders of the movement and placed hundreds of others under detention. The revolution of 1848 in Moldavia was over before it had begun.

Paradoxically, the Moldavian failure and frustration of 1848 was reversed the following year when Gregory Ghica, a Unionist and supporter of the 1848 reform programme, was appointed Prince of Moldavia by the Sultan. Together with other reformists, he introduced an agenda that dealt with law and order, education, a relaxation of censorship and abolition of Roma slavery. An advocate of the unification of the Two Principalities, two years after his death in France, Ghica's dream was realized when the double election of Alexandru Cuza in 1859 as Prince of both Moldavia and Wallachia provided the Romanians with a single ruler for the first time in the modern era along with real autonomy guaranteed by the great powers. Two years later the actual administrative unification of the two principalities became a reality.

Nation building came at a price for Moldavia. The new Romanian capital of Bucharest in Wallachia with its imported German monarch, Karl Hohenzollern-Sigmaringen, his German wife, Elizabeth of Wied, and his nephew Ferdinand as Crown Prince, had little resonance with Iaşi and Cernăuți in the faraway north-east. Bessarabia, which had been returned to Moldavia after the Crimean War, changed hands yet again at the end of the Russo-Turkish War of 1877–78 when it was re-annexed by Russia.

Still predominantly an agrarian society dominated by absentee landlords who delegated the running of their estates to managers to collect rents and enforce bad debts[11], the oil revenues that swelled the tax take in Bucharest bypassed these Eastern borderlands. In 1907, a peasants' revolt broke out in northern Moldavia and rapidly spread to Wallachia. Their grievances were simple. The reforms of 1864 when peasants had been given full ownership rights to lands they had previously only had a right to use had proved inadequate. A rising peasant population coupled with reluctance by landowners to sell land collided with a dramatic fall in the world price of grain. The reaction of the state defied the norms of contemporary governance in Western Europe; several thousand civilians were killed by troops sent in to quash the revolt.

Romania had managed to remain neutral for the first two years of the Great War, but by August 1916 it was clear that an alliance with the Entente was in its best interests, so in exchange for the Allies recognising the rights of Romania over Transylvania, the Banat and Bucovina and

---

[11] According to the 1803 Moldavian census, out of the 1,711 villages and market towns, the boyars owned 927 of them. Little had changed in the way of ownership during the 19th century.

official recognition for the union of these territories with the Kingdom of Romania at a post-war peace conference, Romania agreed to launch an offensive against the Central Powers. The King declared war on 27 August 1916 and on that same day Romanian troops crossed the Carpathians into Transylvania. Then the initial gains and the sense of elation that went with them abruptly stalled.

German and Austrian Hungarian armies embarked on a masterly counterattack. By October, the Romanian army had been comprehensively defeated; three quarters of the territory of the Romanian kingdom was under enemy occupation. In addition, British military engineers had set fire to Romania's oil fields and refineries to deny their use to the enemy. At the beginning of 1917, Moldavia became the centre of resistance, for the Russian army had belatedly managed to stabilise the front in southern Moldavia, giving the Romanians the opportunity to regroup. A new government of national unity was formed in Iaşi. Conditions were grim as thousands of refugees from the occupied territories flooded into the area in the middle of winter. An outbreak of typhoid fever spread rapidly. Communist agitators planned to assassinate the King and Queen. To boost morale and secure the loyalty of the peasants, in July 1917 King Ferdinand and the new Brătianu government shrewdly issued proclamations promising agrarian reform and universal voting rights although they were not to take effect until after the war.

At the same time, strenuous efforts were undertaken to rebuild the virtually decimated Romanian army. This task was given to a French military mission headed by General Henri Berthelot, which had arrived in Romania the previous October. Together with the Romanian general staff, he succeeded in creating a new fully operational army of some 20 divisions totalling half a million soldiers, most of which were active by June of 1917. However, the strategic situation had changed with the outbreak of the Russian revolution in March 1917. The German high command launched a general offensive in the summer designed to defeat Romania once and for all, and to consolidate the Danube Carpathian front against Russia.

However, this time they were in for a surprise for the Romanian army, although inadequately supported by its Russian allies, held on throughout July and August and fought the Germans to a standstill. From a strategic point of view, it was a victory. The great battle of Mărăşesti saved the Romanian kingdom, redeemed Romania in the eyes of the Allies and marked the last German offensive in the sector. The pressure now mounted for the Central Powers to make a separate peace with the Romanians. Its Western allies could not offer any substantial assistance, and Russia was nearing completion of the Treaty of Brest-Litovsk, which would effectively eliminate the Eastern front, so in February 1918 Romania capitulated and reluctantly reached an onerous peace agreement with the Central Powers. From then on it was out of the war until 1 December 1918 when the king and queen accompanied by General Berthelot re-entered Bucharest at the head of their battered but victorious army.

The outcome of the Great War for Moldavia was nothing less than momentous. Bessarabia was reunited with Moldavia and likewise Bucovina once again became part of the old principality. But the great prize for Romania was the unification with Transylvania, which was promulgated on 24 December 1918. From the ashes of a near fatal defeat, the modern Romanian nation state had emerged, and a new page in the history of the Romanians had been turned. The pre-war Romanian kingdom had comprised a territory of 120,000 square kilometres and seven and a half million people. It now entered the interwar period with a territory of 295,000 square kilometres and sixteen million people.

Paddy later became fascinated with the history of Moldavia and its revolving borders when he co-authored *Trials and Tribulations of a Tumbleweed: the Memoirs of Prince Michel Cantacuzène, Count Spéransky.*

BĂLENI

'...the long Moldavian manor houses, close to their counterparts in the novels of Turgenev, were scattered like a dispersed fleet of white ships.'

~ Words of Mercury

The next stage of Paddy's Romanian adventure took place in the febrile and at times frenzied political drama that unfolded in the run up to the Second World War. Scarcely a day passed without news of catastrophe and upheaval in Europe and rumours of unrest and plots abounded in the lobbies of Bucharest's hotels. Both Olivia Manning in *Fortunes of War* and Rosie Waldeck in *Athene Palace* brilliantly capture the atmosphere of intrigue and suspicion that radiated out from the Royal Palace.

When he first returned to Romania in May 1935, the political landscape had once again changed; this time the Iron Guard was centre stage for German interest in the Legion had begun to develop and it was widely believed that the Nazi party was now funding it. In the elections of November 1937, Codreanu's All for The Fatherland Party won 16% of the vote, making it the third largest. Of more concern was the fact that the governing party, Tatarescu's Liberal Party, had for the first time in the history of Romanian democracy failed to amass 40% of the vote. That Christmas the traditional lighting of the Royal tree was cancelled.

By February 1938, it looked like the country was heading for a civil war between the Legion and the Goga/Cuza government's blue-shirted Lăncieri with Romania's Jews caught in the middle after a raft of anti-Semitic decrees were announced. Within months, the situation had deteriorated to the point when King Carol dissolved all political parties and organizations and proclaimed a new constitution, in effect a Royal dictatorship with control vested in the Crown Council. Codreanu was summarily arrested and put on trial.

Then came news in July that the terminally-ill Queen Marie, the Queen Mother, had returned to Romania from hospital in Germany to die. At her state funeral in Bucharest, over a quarter of a million people lined the mauve-draped streets to pay their respects to their beloved English Queen who had taken them to her heart and led them in the dark days of the First World War.

In November 1938, Codreanu and thirteen other Legionnaires, who had been found guilty of treason and imprisoned, were executed by the government in a macabre ritual of strangulation followed by internment in acid and the concreting over of their burial site. That December, Carol felt strong enough to announce his Front of National Rebirth, a single political party to govern Romania under his Kingship.

This time as he crossed the border into Romania, Paddy was not alone but in the company of his lover, the beautiful and artistic Princess Marie-Blanche ['Balaşa'] Cantacuzino, on their way to stay at her country home at Băleni on the rolling Moldavian Bugeac steppe after spending the summer together in an old watermill overlooking the Saronic Gulf in Greece. Balaşa , who was born in July 1899, and her sister Elena ['Pomme'], born the following year, were the daughters of Prince Leon Cantacuzino, a Moldavian landowner whose family came from one of the great Romanian political dynasties that over the centuries had provided both Princes and statesmen for both Wallachia and Moldavia.

The descendants of the Byzantine Emperor John VI Kantakouzenos[1] [ruled 1347–1354], they arrived in the Romanian lands after the

---

[1] Donald Nicol's study *The Byzantine family of Kantakouzenos* goes into great detail.

fall of Constantinople in 1453 and it was the sons of Andronikos Kantakouzenos, a 16th century Phanariot financier and 'mare vistiernic' to Prince Michael the Brave, who founded the two branches of the family in the Principalities. The Moldavian side of the family included Prince Dumitrașcu Cantacuzino, who ruled briefly on three separate occasions in 17th century, Prince Gheorghe Cantacuzino, Great Treasurer of Moldavia in 1633 and a number of Chancellors.

The Băleni branch of the family began when Prince Matei Cantacuzino, the Grand Vornic and Vistiar of Moldavia, and his family decamped to Russia in 1791 to escape the clutches of the Ottomans[2]. Like Dimitrie Cantemir a century before, Matei calculated that the future of Moldavia was best entrusted to Moscow for the Habsburgs, who had annexed Bucovina in 1765, had shown scant respect for the Principality's institutions and little regard for its Orthodox heritage. His son, Alexandru [1781–1841], became Chamberlain to the Tsar and a general in the Russian army[3], distinguishing himself in the Greek War of Independence when he oversaw the surrender of the old Byzantine stronghold of Monemvasia in the Peloponnese. It was his grandson, Gheorghe[4] [1840–1911] who moved to the estate at Băleni[5] and subsequently handed it on to his son Leon, Balașa's father, in 1891.

Leon married Anne Văcărescu who came from one of the oldest boyar families in Wallachia[6]. Her niece, Ana Maria Văcărescu-Callimachi remembered[7] her as 'a type of perfect snob…keen on keeping in step with the latest fashion'. With a luxurious trousseau to her name, she had married 'a half-princely Russian who was extremely wealthy and very different from his father [Gheorghe] who was in the true sense a noble prince – tall, blonde and with a beard who never travelled without water from his own wells and his campaign bed'. If Gheorghe had a weakness, it was for the extravagantly cut clothes of the 1830s.

Ana Maria was scathing of Leon, who 'had not inherited anything from

---

[2] He was by no means the only Cantacuzino to head East. Ioan Cantacuzino [1757–1828], knighted by Catherine the Great for his services in the Russo-Turkish War of 1787–1792, was given land on the River Bug where he founded the village of Kantakuzinka, now in the Ukraine.

[3] This line of the family later received the title Count Speransky and were confirmed as princely rank in Russia in 1893.

[4] Gheorghe was born in Dresden and married Fanny Beer.

[5] Băleni had come into the family in 1835 through his mother, Aristita Ghika.

[6] NLS Acc.13338/342.

[7] Conacul de la Mănești prinde viată, Magazin Istoric October 2003.

his father except his money which he gambled away or spent in the company of attractive women, preferably French actresses'. Indeed, the names of every charming girl were to be found in his cheque book. Although a Member of Parliament, 'his conversation was extremely bland, especially when politics were discussed for he knew almost nothing'. Perhaps it was just as well that both girls were educated by an English governess, Miss Violet Williamson[8], and then sent to a finishing school in Brighton, for two of Balaşa's books are annotated Brighton 1912 and Brighton 1914.

Ethel Pantazzi, the Canadian wife of a Romanian Naval Captain who was in charge of the port at Galaţi, was asked to join a house party at Băleni in October 1914 when the guest of honour was no less than Queen Marie, 'the very embodiment of beauty and romance'. She wrote of returning from the vineyards through a 'very civilized' forest with 'our conveyances decorated with crimson and yellow autumn leaves'. In the evening *jeux d'esprit* were the diversion. The park was illuminated with Chinese lanterns and spirited tzigane music made her toes tingle.[9]

When Balaşa's grandfather Gheorghe died in Alexandria in Egypt in November 1910, her father set off to repatriate his body. Three weeks later, on 3 December, officiated over by Archbishop Nifon, his funeral took place at Băleni. Among the mourners, *La Roumanie* reported, were devoted servants, local dignitaries and 'une grande affluence de paysans'. In addition to the immediate family, the list of those attending reflected the links of the Cantacuzino-Băleni and extended Cantacuzino family throughout Romania and beyond – Deym-Schtretitz, Grabcewska, Ghyka-Deleni, Stârcea, Greceano, Mourousi, Bellio, Polizo-Micşuneşti, Vacaresco, Soutzo, O'Donnel, Schoborn, Krupensky, Kotzebue, Donici, Sturdza, Catargi, Balsh, Callimachi and many others.

In June 1920, the British Royal family held their first 'court' since 1913. *The Times* reported how 'the Palace's gates were thrown open and guests began to pour in'. One such guest was 21-year-old 'Mademoiselle Marie Blanche

---

[8] One of the books from Băleni in the V.A.Urechia library is inscribed Violet Williamson 1906; another book inscribed 'with love from Mr Jamie, 21 March 1913' shows an address in London, 11 Cornwall Avenue, Church End, Finchley. According to the 1911 census, this was the home of Jamie and Jane Martindale. Jane's sister was married to Major Williamson, Violet's brother; a passport to travel to Romania was issued to Violet on 29 June 1914 [TNA: FO 655/1039].

[9] Ethel Paltazzi: *Roumania in light and shade.*

Cantacuzene' who was presented by H.E. Madame Merry de Val[10]. From then on, Balaşa was never short of admirers of all ages. The courtier Lord Kintore[11] writing to her from the Carlton Club on 20 July 1921 described how his 'old heart jumped with joy this morning when after an absolutely airless night with excessive heat I came to my letters on my breakfast table and saw a letter with two Romanian stamps on it'[12]. In another letter he muses 'how I should really love to find myself arriving there in Galatz[13] on my way to pay you a little visit. Do the Danube steamers run all the long way from Hungary to Galatz? If I was in Bucharest first could I come thence to you by train?'[14]

Both her parents died in 1923, her father ironically in Egypt like Gheorghe. Her sister Pomme had been given Băleni by their father soon after the death of his wife in March. Even after the agrarian reforms of 1921, it was still a substantial estate of over 2,850 hectares, notwithstanding the considerable debts she had also inherited from her wastrel father[15].

The following year, Balaşa married a handsome Spanish diplomat, 27-year-old Francisco ['Paco'] de Amat y Torres, who was serving in Bucharest as a third secretary: postings soon followed to Warsaw, Madrid, Belgrade and then to Athens. It was here in 1932 that the marriage came apart. According to some reports, Paco fell in love with Clothilde[16], the American wife of British diplomat Billy Cavendish-Bentinck, later 9th Duke of Portland. However, in 1947, *The Times* published a report on the divorce[17] proceedings of the Bentincks in which a different version of events emerged.

Estranged from his wife for nearly ten years and wanting to marry his

---

[10] Maria Merry del Val née Alzol (1879–1959), wife of Don Alfonso Merry del Val, Spanish Ambassador to England 1913–1931.

[11] Algernon Keith-Falconer, the 9th Earl, was 68 years old at the time of correspondence.

[12] NLS Acc.13338/129.

[13] German spelling of Galați.

[14] NLS Acc.13338/129.

[15] The Donicis had to remortgage the estate in 1927 to pay down the outstanding debts.

[16] Clothilde Quigley was the daughter of a prominent Kentucky lawyer. Her mother had taken her and her sister to Paris in 1923 where she met Billy who was resident secretary at the Embassy. He proposed much against the wishes of his family and they married the following year.

[17] Clothilde left her husband at the beginning of the war and took her two children to America. They were finally divorced in 1948.

long-standing mistress Kathleen Tillotson, Bentinck had brought divorce proceedings against Clothilde on the ground of her adultery with Paco. She denied it and alleged desertion and adultery on the part of Billy. On 27 March 1947, the judge, Mr Justice Hodson, listened to the 'frank evidence' in which Billy disclosed his adultery with 'a series of mistresses' and 'three extra-marital adventures of an isolated character'. The first of the mistresses, in 1932, was the wife of the co-respondent, none other than Balaşa. The second mistress was acquired in Chile in 1935, his next Foreign Office posting.

With such damaging admissions, Clothilde's KC soon persuaded the judge that, given she had been very strictly brought up, his client was probably only playing with the idea she was in love with Paco and enjoyed his admiration. Letters which Paco had written to her in 1936 when he was fighting in the Spanish Civil War were deemed 'consistent with a non-adulterous relationship' and the fact that Paco was in California at the same time as Clothilde in 1942 mere coincidence. The judge dismissed Billy's charges and granted Clothilde a judicial separation[18].

In the ensuing scandal, there were serious ramifications for Cavendish-Bentinck who had played a major role in British intelligence during the war as Chairman of the newly formed Joint Intelligence Committee and later as a co-author of the Bland Report[19]. Nominated on 21 February on his return from Poland, where he had been Ambassador, as the next British Ambassador to Brazil, the Foreign Office publicly cancelled his appointment on 15 April and thus marked a humiliating end to his distinguished diplomatic career. Not only was he deprived of his career but also of all his pension rights. The hand of Ernest Bevin was evident; he reputedly told his Private Secretary 'I could have saved him if his name had been Smith'.[20] By the time Billy appealed in November 1947 and been vindicated by the judge who accepted his claim that Clothilde and Paco had been lovers was true, the damage had been done.

Whatever the truth, Balaşa's marriage was annulled in Rome in 1927[21]. Paco returned to Spain while Balaşa remained in Athens and it was here she met Paddy in the summer of 1935. By the autumn, they were liv-

---

[18] *The Times*, 27 March 1947; Lady Margaret Graubard: *In the best society* p.248. She was Billy and Clothilde's daughter.

[19] *The Future Organization of the S.I.S*, 12 October 1944.

[20] Patrick Howarth: *Intelligence Chief Extraordinary*, p.222.

[21] Balaşa still signed her name as Balaşa de Amat in November 1927 in a book now in the V.A. Urechia library.

ing at the *conac* [22] in Băleni, together with Balaşa's sister Pomme and her husband Constantin Donici.

A gentle fay character, this tall slim woman with slender expressive arms, possessed almond eyes set beneath a broad forehead and observed the world around her with a curious friendly gaze. She embraced painting and poetry as her media of self-expression and was the perfect foil for the exuberant and precocious young Paddy. As he wrote years later[23], 'it would be impossible to fit these two sisters into any category. Sent to school in France and England and finished and brought out all over the place, they were good, beautiful, courageous, gifted, imaginative, immersed in literature and the arts, kind, funny and unconventional; everybody loved them, and so did I.' In a letter to Balaşa written in 1965, he recalled 'it was really the beginning of life for me, and changed everything'.[24]

In late spring 1936, Paddy set out to visit the Danube Delta with Balaşa's cousin and neighbor Alexandru Moruzi[25] of Golásei. In *Journey Down the Danube*[26], Paddy returned to the Delta 'the Black Sea's enormous green antechamber' and remembered 'fragments of my former wanderings [as they] dropped about me in a soft impressionable rain: Vâlcov spread a maze of little canals and plank bridges and catwalks in a haze of reeds and bamboos and willows where the heretical domes of the Lippovans floated like a flimsey Venice…Shadowy Gothic journeys unwind for days along tunnels of reed that expand without warning in wide glades of weed and water flowers…and the lagoons reflect tall woods of birch and aspen and poplar and a fluttering infinity of green and silver leaves and drooping pavilions of willow…'

He explained how he and Alexandru Moruzi 'went to Galaţi by train [from Băleni], then by river steamer up the northernmost tributary of the river to the beautiful little amphibious town of Vâlcov, a maze of willow-shaded canals and White Russian fishermen who, every few hours, landed enormous sturgeon from whose vast slimy bellies troves of caviar were untimely ripped'. Having met up with Nikolai, a Lippovan, they 'set off eastwards in his *lotka* through a maze of minor branches of the great

---

[22] The nearest word in English is a country or manor house.

[23] *Daily Telegraph Weekend Magazine*, 12 May 1990.

[24] NLS Acc.13338/129–134 Letter PLF to Balaşa Cantacuzino 20 April 1965.

[25] Descendant of Prince Alexandru Moruzi, Grand Dragoman of the Sublime Porte (1790–92), Prince of Moldavia (1793–96 and 1799–1801) and Prince of Wallachia (1792, 1801–06 and 1806–07). Also spelt Mourousi, Morouzi and Muruzi.

[26] NLS Acc.13338/208.

river, across wide lagoons and down endless winding watery corridors of ostrich-plumed reeds twenty feet high that seemed to waft us along with their murmuring...It was without exception the strangest region I have ever seen...Nikolai, unerringly every night, would steer us to some reef in this reedy wilderness, a remote dune where, living in stilted houses like samovars, a colony of his fellow Lippovans would welcome us among the net-looped willows'.

In *Western from the city; Journey from Constantinople to Adrianople*, Paddy completes the story of how they returned to Bucharest where Alexandru borrowed some money from a rich uncle and they treated themselves to lunch at Capşas before retiring to 'the leafy delights of high Moldavia, the long rides through the oak woods full of hoopoes and bee-eaters and golden orioles, to books and poetry and freezing wine and dinner and mosquitoless conversation by candlelight in shadowy gardens...'

Later that summer he went with Balaşa to see the painted churches of the Bucovina[27]. If only he had crafted for us one of those soaring pen paintings of the little 16th century painted churches at Voroneţ or Humor, of the exquisite frescoes that hide behind the great walls of Suceviţa and Moldoviţa. These painted churches on the farthest edge of Byzantium, still caught in the glow of the art and learning of Constantinople, must have enthralled him as much Sacherverell Sitwell, who found Voroneţ 'one of the marvels of the Byzantine world', comparable to Patmos, Santorini and Meteora. In his chapter on ikons in *Mani*, Paddy outpours the historical knowledge of the Orthodox tradition he has both acquired and spiritually absorbed. Surely some of the seeds of this enlightenment were sown in the Bucovina, perhaps at Suceviţa where 'barely sheltered from snow and rain by a loggia on the outer walls of remote fanes, the weatherworn lineaments of the pagan sages of the Greek world can be discerned: Solon, Plato, Aristotle, Plutarch, Thucydides, Sophocles and Apollonius of Tyana, arrayed in robes as honorable as those that adorn the Christian saints, but bereft of haloes'[28].

From Bucovina, they travelled to Bessarabia, today part Moldova and part Ukraine. In 1994, writing[29] to Michael Cantacuzène, Paddy recalled 'just before the war, we went, largely on horseback, to see a lot of

---

[27] Artemis Cooper: *Paddy Leigh Fermor, An Adventure.*

[28] *The Mani,* Chapter 15.

[29] NLS Acc.13338/334–343 Letter PLF to Michael Cantacuzène 17 March 1994.

Cantacuzene and Krupensky[30] relations beyond the Prut River along the Dniester in Bessarabia and feasted under trees at Novoe Usadba, the house of dear old general Volodia [Vladimir] Kantakuzin[31]...before moving on to another crumbling Krupenski gentilhommière called Lamashnitza. Happy days!' Vladimir, a former general of Horse Artillery in the Russian army, wounded at Port Arthur in the Russo-Japanese war and in the Great War when fighting for Austro-Hungary, had joined Admiral Alexander Kolchak's White army in Siberia after the Revolution. After a lucky escape, he lived with one of his sisters at Noua Usadba on the Lencăuti estate that bordered the Dnieper river in Jud Hotin in Bessarabia. Such were the swings of history that, on his return to the newly Romanian-owned Bessarabia, Vladimir 'became Romanian after a century of Russification'[32].

Country life in Moldavia was punctuated by visits to England. In January 1937 Paddy and Balaşa stayed with the Branchs in Pembroke Square[33] and then rented a flat in Earl's Court. Through Balaşa's friend Costa Achillopoulos, Paddy met Sacheverell and Georgia Sitwell who were to become his lifelong friends. In May, Balaşa was invited by the Royal Romanian Legation as an official guest to attend the Coronation Naval Review at Spithead, the first since 1912, but the frenetically social English summer season was no substitute for the romantic rusticity of the water-mill at Lemonodassos. Soon the two lovers decamped to Greece, travelling by boat from Marseilles after visiting friends in France[34].

Visitors to Băleni included some of Romanians leading intellectuals and artists such as the polymath and raconteur Georges Cantacuzino who left an indelible impression on the young Paddy. Painter, architect, politician, urban planner, historian and author, Georges and his wife, Sanda [the niece of Barbu Ştirbey], both in their 30s, epitomized civilized Romanian society. During Paddy's stay, Georges juggled his duties as Director of Architecture for Romanian Railways with designing and constructing the Romanian Pavilion at the World Fair in New York, a project personally

---

[30] The Krupensky family owned vast estates around Hotin and Soccata. Mihail [1851–1905] and Alexandr [1861–1939] were both Marshal of the Nobility of the Bessarabia *gubernia* before Bessarabia was returned to Romania in 1919.

[31] Married to Sophia Mitru Nicolaevitch, he had four children.

[32] Mihai dim Sturdza: *History of the Cantacuzinos.*

[33] It is not clear how they met. In 1939 Guy married Lady Prudence Pelham [daughter of 6th Earl of Chichester] whose family home, Stanmer Park, was close to Brighton. There is a suggestion that Balaşa may have stayed there when she was studying in Brighton before the First World War.

[34] Artemis Cooper: *Paddy Leigh Fermor, An Adventure.*

supervised by King Carol, as well as managing his own thriving prestigious architectural practice in Bucharest. As if this was not enough to occupy him, an account of his extensive travels to the Holy Land, the Levant, Mesopotamia and Persia was published as *Patrar de Veghe* in 1938 and an arts review *Simetria* launched by him the following year.

Another figure who dazzled Paddy was Prince Matila Ghyka, novelist, naval officer, mathematician, historian, philosopher, and diplomat who became Minister Plenipotentiary in London in the late 1930s. Twenty years older than Cantacuzino, the two men were both descendants of famous Moldavian ruling families and firm friends through their interests in the arts and science. As Paddy wrote in his introduction to Ghyka's memoir in 1961, 'the charm, intelligence, humour and fun and the range and the stimulus of conversations in Moldavia equaled anything I can remember since'. Ghyka loved Băleni, 'a faraway refuge, many miles from anywhere, of beauty, intelligence, originality and kindness. A peculiar and potent magic pervaded this house and all its inhabitants'[35].

In 1938, Ghyka's wife Eileen and their two children, Maureen 18 and Roderick 15, spent the summer at Băleni with Balaşa and Pomme. Matila remembered the staff consisted of 'a cook, an octogenarian maid-of-all-work, rich in proverbs and folk tales, a retired Polish coachman called Pani, a Ukrainian butler called Ilfin who floated in a soft and vinuous haze, and a befezzed Turk called Mustapha.' The house 'standing among tall trees, was long and rambling. Meals were at all hours, and thanks to an abundance of hare, partridge and quail, the meals were varied and delicious. The vineyard of the now very shrunken estate produced a once famous wine… Life ebbed gently away at Băleni with reading and chess and endless talks at night, and I was reminded of my childhood summers at Dumbraveni[36]'.

By way of speculation, it is probable that Paddy also met Princess Maruca Cantacuzino[37]. 'With her ethereal albeit dark beauty, tall slender body, and large, dreamy black eyes'[38], this widowed 'Byzantine beauty' as Matila Ghyka described her – her late husband had been the Minister of Justice in 1910 – was at the centre of *un triangle amoreux* with the philosopher Nae Ionescu and the composer George Enescu whom she later married. Her daughter Alice, who was married to Mihail Sturdza, was an

---

[35] Matila Ghyka: *The World Mine Oyster.*

[36] A vast Ghyka estate of 60,000 acres, 14 villages and three huge forests near Botoşani in northern Moldavia.

[37] Née Rosetti-Teţcanu, she had married Mihail Cantacuzino, son of the fabulously wealthy 'Nabob' Cantacuzino.

[38] Anne-Marie Callimachi: *Yesterday was Mine.*

exact contemporary of Balaşa and shared her love of the arts although she was of a literary bent rather than a painter. In the slim portfolio of Balaşa's pictures that survived the post-war depredations there is a 1938 sketch of Maruca's house at Teţcanu.

The family of Nicky Chrissoveloni, Paddy's banking[39] friend from his stay in Bucharest, also owned a large late 19th century French-style mansion at Ghidigeni, about 35 miles from Băleni. *Palatul* Chrissoveloni or The Palace of Pleasure as it was known had been notorious at one stage for its lavish parties attended by King Ferdinand. Later, during the First World War, Nicky's English mother Sybille with the support of Queen Marie transformed it into The Prince Mircea Hospital for wounded soldiers. With visitors such as the prominent politicians Grigore Gafencu and Constantin Argetoianu, the fabulously wealthy trader George Negroponte and the architect Georges Cantacuzino, who had designed the bank's head office at 17 Lipscani Street in Bucharest, Balaşa and Paddy were surely on the guest list of the Chrissovelonis. In a post-war photograph, Balaşa can be seen standing next to George Lakeman-Economu[40], whose daughter Georgeta was married to Nicky. Ina Donici is in the foreground, trying to restrain their infant daughter Sybill from crawling out of the picture.

When Paddy and Balaşa returned to Romania in the spring of 1938, the political landscape had irrevocably changed; Carol had crushed the Iron Guard and announced his Front of National Rebirth, in effect a royal dictatorship, a very Romanian compromise that was neither 'neither a tyranny nor totalitarian regime'[41]. The extended Cantacuzino family had been swept up by the waves of political extremity. General Gheorghe Cantacuzino-Grănicerul, holder of Romania's highest military honour the Order of St Michael the Brave, had deputized for Codreanu as the leader of The All for The Fatherland Party and had been imprisoned from December 1933 to April 1934. At his funeral on 12 October 1937, the Romanian Army had marched at the head of his cortège in Bucharest while Codreanu's Iron Guard brought up the rear. Prince Alexandru Cantacuzino, one of Codreanu's right hand men, was arrested and then murdered by police in

---

[39] The Chrissoloveni Bank had collapsed in 1931 after a run but had been restarted in 1936 with help of Hambros Bank in London.

[40] George was the son of Sir Stephen Bartlett Lakeman, an extraordinary Anglo-Dutch soldier of fortune who had been knighted by Queen Victoria for his military services in Africa and then appointed by the Ottoman Sultan as governor of Bucharest in 1854. Known as Mazar Pasha, he was instrumental in the disengagement process between the United Provinces and the Porte and was a co-founder of the Romanian Liberal Party in 1875.

[41] Armin Heinen

1939 after the killing of Prime Minister Călinescu and the courageous Princess Ioana Cantacuzino, the first woman to hold a pilot's licence in Romania, was imprisoned for a year in 1940 in the Târgu-Jiu concentration camp after falling out with Marshal Antonescu.

That summer, Guy Branch's 19-year-old sister Biddy[42] came to stay at Băleni. It was her first holiday abroad on her own and what could be more romantic than this entrée into the secret world of the boyars nestled in a fold of the great Moldavian prairie. 'The long, low, white house lay in the sunshine like a sunken ship. The shutters were green and the shadow of the acacia trees speckled the walls…The summer is nearly over: the earth under the trees was pale and dry, the few flowers withered. On one side of the house lay a biblical rolling plain, the landscape stretched and bare, with mauve shadows that were always beaten dry clay when you reached them. Blonde oxen pulled carts along fawn-coloured roads which had no borders and dissolved into the dust of the plain'[43].

Her hostess, Balaşa , is observed 'drifting dreamily through the rooms with that swaying walk…How did it feel to be dark and beautiful and 35, to have been married to a Spaniard, to live sometimes here in Moldavia as a feudal aristocrat, a boyar, with your brother and sister-in-law , sometimes in London with a young English lover and no money?' On one occasion, Balaşa insisted that they drive miles to have dinner with Alexandru Moruzi, 'a bachelor friend who lived alone…his house was large and white with Corinthian pillars. Romantic, fantastic, decaying'.

Biddy gives an account of an expedition to the Bucovina. There were five passengers in the old Ford driven by Constantin – Pomme and her daughter Ina who looked like Millais' Ophelia[44], Balaşa, Paddy and Biddy Branch herself. The first night was spent in the garden of Agapia Monastery '…occupied by silent dark nuns with white cast-down moonish faces, kneeling like beetles in the candle-lit church'. Most likely the party stayed in one or two of the little guesthouses that clutter the walled monastery garden. The following day, after visiting the great 15th century monastery at Neamţ and the Secu Monastery at the foot of Vasan mountain, in the afternoon they stopped to watch a peasant wedding party, then joined in the traditional *hora* dance, 'stumping round and round on the grass learning new steps and laughing…A fat glowing girl taught Michael [Paddy] the polka'.

[42] Biddy married Thomas Hubbard in 1939 and died in 2017, aged 99.

[43] NLS Acc.13338/272.

[44] *Daily Telegraph Weekend Magazine*, 12 May 1990.

Finally they reached the exquisitely painted church exteriors of Voroneț and Moldovița the next day, 'dream-like Byzantine buildings from a fairy story'[45].

Another first-hand account of 1938 is provided by the author and playwright Derek Patmore. Like Sacheverell Sitwell, he had been enticed by Princess Anne-Marie Callimachi to write a travel book about Romania, all expenses paid by the Romanian Government. Rather than go direct, Patmore decided to travel via Italy and Greece and it was in Athens that he met up with Balașa and Paddy. 'I had known Balașa in London', he recalled in *Private History*, '…a striking Byzantine beauty with enormous dark eyes and a pale skin'. Since they were 'very much in love, and had little money', he invited them to come to Delphi with him as his guests, together with the celebrated fashion photographer Baron George von Hoyningen-Huene who was the lover of Horst, his photographic assistant and model.

In *Images of Greece*, Patmore is more circumspect and merely refers to visiting Delphi with two friends, 'one a young Englishman, Paddy Leigh-Fermor, the other a gifted Rumanian artist, Balașa Cantacuzene'. In 'the scent of late summer [when] the fall of the year was everywhere', they set off early one morning by bus from Athens and after a seven-hour journey during which 'a large gentleman kept falling asleep on the shoulder of my English friend, Paddy', they arrived in Delphi where they met the young 29-year-old French archaeologist Etienne Coche De La Ferté[46] whom Patmore found fascinating. The next day, 'when the shadows began to cover the place with a brooding darkness, we left the little town nestling against its majestic mountains and drove to the nearest station to take the train back to Athens'.

Paddy must have been impressed by being included in this group of celebrities. The versatile and gregarious 30-year-old Patmore, a friend of Eddie Marsh and Norman Douglas among many others, had co-written *Life of a Lady: A Play in Three Acts* with the poet Richard Aldington in 1936. Equally at home in the literary milieu of Paris and Florence where his mother lived, he had dexterously reinvented himself as an interior decorator in New York and had just had his first design book, *I Decorate My Home,* published by Harpers. A mix of German and American parentage, Russian-born George von Hoyningen-Huene, who had been the chief photographer at *Vogue* in Paris, had recently moved to New York where he was working for *Harpers Bazaar*.

---

[45] NLS Acc.13338/272 From a fragment of a manuscript by Biddy.

[46] De La Ferté became a writer in later life, best known as the biographer of Hugo Von Hofmannstahl and the history of *L'Art de Byzance*.

In *Invitation to Romania*, Patmore visits Balaşa's cousin Alexandru Moruzi for dinner at Golásei. He has two surprises, the first a gypsy orchestra from the village and the second a consignment of caviar which arrives by special train from Galaţi. The evening finished with dancing in 'the great room…servant girls, looking very pretty in their gaily coloured costumes, swirled around the floor in the intricate steps of the Roumanian dances…Caught by the wild music, Balaşa and Paddy got up and danced with the rest, and this gave an added impetus to the dancing…The room was hot. So Alexander opened one of the windows and we went and stood on the wide terrace outside. It was a clear moonlit night, and the silver light made the white façade of the house gleam with a ghostly radiance.'

When news came the next morning [15 September] of the crisis in Czechoslovakia, Paddy drove Patmore to the station in an old-fashioned horse-drawn carriage. 'It was dark already, and as we drove along, a stormy wind had blown up from the east. It blew great clouds of dust all around us, and made the dark countryside appear very abandoned and forlorn. It was very dark. The carry had only two candle-lamps in front, and as the wind howled around us and the harness of the horses jangled in front, it seemed as if we were in an old Russian novel. There was that same sense of vast, dark landscapes and that inescapable fate which pursues the destiny of man'[47]. Patmore returned the following year for there is a copy of his book, *Colour Schemes for the Modern Home*, in the V.A. Urechia library in Galaţi inscribed 'For dear Pom [sic], in memory of my pleasant days at Băleni. How nice to find one of one's books so far from England! Derek Patmore, Băleni, 29 June 1939'.

It was at Băleni in September 1939 that Paddy learnt of the outbreak of war and returned to England to enlist. In his introduction to Matila Ghyka's *The World Mine Oyster* in 1961, he recalled Băleni as 'a faraway refuge of beauty, intelligence, originality and kindness'. Then like a magician, he transports us to a fairytale place where 'at night we dined under the trees with the moon slanting through the branches overhead, the talk falling silent now and then to look up at shooting stars or to listen to a nightingale. Once or twice, far into the night, gypsies would come with their violins and play and sing until the fading candles and the blue-green light that stole through the tree trunks would tell us that the sun was rising out of Bessarabia'.

His description of the return of the mushroom-gathering picnic

---

[47] Derek Patmore: *Invitation to Romania*.

poignantly recalls 'a moment of peace and tranquility' as the party passed 'homing peasants waving their hats in greeting' as the flocks streamed 'in haloes of golden dust to the wells' while 'a blurred line along the sky a league away marked the itinerary of the deserting storks'. Unknown but not unexpected, the news of war the next day, 3 September 1939, 'scattered this little society for-ever'. Paddy left the next day, together with Henry Nevile[48], Eileen Ghyka's nephew who had been staying at Băleni. A long affectionate letter from Balaşa dated 26 October 1940[49] reached him in England. The news was not good. 'Ma Cherie, Je suis au près de toi bien souvent. The Russian border is now 5 kms away, the horses have all been requisitioned and also the car…Je t'aime, je t'embrasse'. Then came a silence enforced by the vicissitudes of a war that lasted for six years.

By November, having been accepted for a commission in the Irish Guards, Paddy had joined a group of other potential officers for training at the Guards Depot in Caterham in Surrey. The course, known as the Brigade Squad, was tough and unrelenting. Hours were spent square-bashing, cleaning kit and preparing lockers and bedspaces for barrack room inspections. An attack of scabies in December meant that Paddy missed over five weeks of training and as a result he did not go on to Sandhurst with the rest of the Squad. Fortuitously as it turned out, he then accepted an offer to join the Intelligence Corps and began his training with them in May. After the Italian invasion of Greece at the end of October, Paddy was posted to the British Military Mission in Athens and soon found himself on the Greek-Albanian border, advising the Greek III Army Corps on 'mountain warfare'.

When Germany invaded Yugoslavia and Greece in April 1941, the recently-arrived British Expeditionary W Force, to which Paddy was now attached, fell back in disarray towards Athens. Retreat or withdrawal as some soldiers prefer to call it is always chaotic and demoralizing and that of W Force was no exception. Making his way south on roads clogged with abandoned vehicles, Paddy reached Athens and from there sailed to Crete on a converted caique. The island was far from a safe haven as it turned out. On 20 May, thousands of German paratroopers descended on the island and in a whirlwind campaign characterized more by British errors than German superiority captured it in its entirety. After being evacuated from

---

[48] Sir Henry Nicholas Nevile, KCVO, KStJ, JP, DL [1920 – 1996].
[49] NLS Acc.13338/129.

Crete by the Royal Navy, Paddy arrived in Egypt and booked into the Continental Hotel in Cairo. Soon he would be back in Crete as an officer of the Special Operations Executive, training and arming the Cretans to take the fight to their Teutonic occupiers. Paddy spent over 18 months living rough in the mountains disguised as a shepherd. When he was finally exfiltrated to Cairo after the dramatic kidnap of the German General Kriepe in May 1944, he was immediately hospitalized, suffering from exhaustion and polyarthritis. His fellow officer Billy Moss recalled in *A War of Shadows*, 'those daily visits to Paddy in hospital – of seeing his arms and fingers growing thinner and thinner, yet swollen and red at the joints...'

Back in Băleni, life had been equally dramatic and far from peaceful. Just as Paddy started his officer training with the Intelligence Corps in Aldershot, the Soviet Union, with the agreement of Germany, delivered a démarche on 26 June 1940 to the Romanian ambassador in Moscow, demanding that Bessarabia and Bucovina be ceded to it. With its allies either overrun or isolated like Britain, the Romanian Government caved in and over the next few days in what was to all extents a full-scale invasion the Russian army entered the eastern provinces. Over 300,000 Romanian refugees trekked westwards and sought shelter in the Old Kingdom; of those who remained nearly 200,000 were deported to Siberia and hundreds of others hunted down and murdered by the NKVD. As for the Romanian Army, it suffered a catastrophic defeat, scarcely firing a shot; some 150,000 soldiers were taken prisoner and a vast amount of war material lost. All these events happened on Balaşa's doorstep and she would have undoubtedly seen or heard about the tattered bands of homeless people shuffling through the village.

This man-made disaster was followed by a devastating earthquake in the early hours of 10 November; the shockwaves at the epicentre in Vrancea County just to the west of Băleni registered 7.7 on the Richter scale, making it the largest earthquake ever recorded in 20th century Romania. The main towns of Focşani, Galaţi and Giurgiu were all seriously damaged; in Bucharest, the 14 storey Carlton block made of reinforced concrete partially collapsed killing 140 people. With the shock wave felt as far away as Budapest and Moscow, it was in many ways surprising that only 600 people died with a further 4,000 injured. The house at Băleni survived although large cracks would have appeared on its walls and many of its windows would have shattered in what must have been a terrifying experience. In 1946, Balaşa told Paddy that her room and 'all that end of the house' had been destroyed.[50]

---

[50] NLS Acc.13338/129–134 Letter Balaşa to PLF dated 27 January 1946.

The loss of Bessarabia and northern Bucovina to Russia had been followed by the far greater national humiliation of the Second Vienna Award when Germany and Italy arbitrarily awarded northern Transylvania to Hungary on 30 August 1940. Greater Romania which had emerged victorious at the end of the Great War lay in fragments, dismantled by Hitler, Mussolini and Stalin. Another 300,000 Romanians streamed into the Old Kingdom in search of shelter and sustenance. This sequence of catastrophic seizures and confiscations marked the end for King Carol who ignominiously fled the country in the royal train. His successor as head of state, Marshal Ion Antonescu, immediately took steps to crush the Iron Guard which Carol had allowed to linger on as part of the body politic and then allied himself with Germany in order to recover the eastern territories stolen by the Russians. On 22 June 1941, days after Paddy arrived in Cairo, the Romanian army crossed the border as part of Operation Barbarossa, the German masterplan to defeat Russia. By 26 July, all the lands of Bessarabia and Bucovina had been recaptured. For the occupants of Băleni and indeed the Romanian people, this return to the status quo ante was an occasion for celebration.

After the earthquake of November 1940 which had destroyed the village church of the Holy Archangels, Constantin and the two Cantacuzino sisters set about building a new one. They gave a parcel of land opposite the *conac* to the diocese in Galați and then launched a charm offensive against officialdom in Bucharest to acquire licenses for building materials that were strictly rationed in wartime. By 1944 the church was completed and it only remained to paint the interior with traditional Orthodox frescoes[51]. Fittingly it was rededicated to St Constantine and St Helena and in the alcove above the west door a plaque to the Donici votives was inserted. When Romania bowed to the inevitable and threw her lot in with the Germans to recover Bessarabia, Balașa volunteered as a nurse and was sent to a military hospital in Bucharest. 'I swept floors and talked to them [the wounded soldiers] about their children and cows and the fig and the weather for crops…it is so awful to use all the best in one's womanhood to put layer and layer of false kindness between death and a man.' She left after a year.[52]

While Paddy lay in his hospital bed in Cairo for three long months, the Russians were massing on the borders of Romania. He had asked Eileen Ghyka for news of Balașa and she wrote to him on 6 June 'last heard of

---

[51] The contents are now in the Ecclesiastical Museum in the Bishop's Palace in Galati.

[52] Ibid Note 91.

B two and a half years ago working in a hospital in Bucharest'[53]. On 20 August, a three million strong Red Army overran Bessarabia and, after the Royal coup that ousted Antonescu and brought the country onto the Allied side, it had occupied most of the country. By 2 September, Russian soldiers had arrived in Băleni.

---

[53] NLS Acc.13338/57.

Balaşa's illustrious ancestor, the Byzantine Emperor John VI Kantacuzenos
[1292–1383]

Prince Gheorghe Cantacuzino

Prince Leon Cantacuzino   *General Volodya Cantacuzino*

Princess Balaşa Cantacuzino

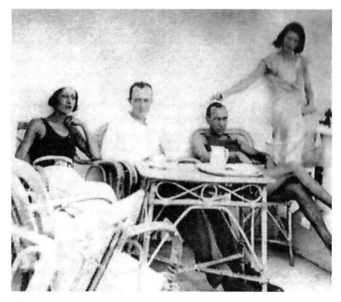

L to R: Balaşa, Bill Bentinck, Paco Amat and Clothilde Bentinck in Greece

Back L to R: Constantin Donici, Balaşa, George Lakeman–Economu, Pomme,
Georgeta and Nicky Chrissoloveni
Front: Ina Donici and Sybill Chrissoloveni

Back L to R: Balaşa, Pomme, Alexandru Moruzi, N/K, Matila Ghyka, Paddy,
Constantin Donici
Front L to R: Roddy Ghyka, Eileen Ghyka, Maureen Ghyka, Ina Donici

The architect Prince Georges Cantacuzino and his pupils

Princess Maruca Cantacuzino

Prince Matila Ghyka

Guy Branch   *Balaşa at Băleni*

Băleni conac

Băleni conac

Băleni conac interior

Cantacuzino family crypt Băleni

Lencăuti

Novoe Usadba

Chrissoloveni palatul at Ghidigeni 1936

Palatul 2017

Georges Cantacuzino's fireplace at Băleni

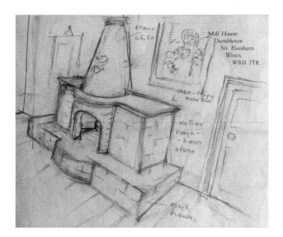

Paddy's sketch

Fireplace at Kardamyli

5 Feb. 2007.

THE MILL HOUSE
DUMBLETON
EVESHAM
WORCESTERSHIRE WR11 6TR
CHELTENHAM 01242 621225

P.S. (This nuisance will soon
cease!)

Marie Lise,

I've just come across this
snap of the Persian fireplace, as
put up in the Mani, based on
my memory of the one we put
up in Balini. The only deviation
from your father's sketch is the
deckle-edged top. ⌐⌐⌐⌐ I suppose
I thought it looked (   ) even more
picturesquely Persian, and it was a
mistake; it is   too high, and, when
a north wind   blows, it smokes
a bit, as the photo   shows.

I think the two wings, on either
side of the arched hearth, had some
heating purpose, a tube or something,
to spread the warmth in the cold
Elburz mountains. Here they are

The 'fireplace' letter to Marie-Lyse Ruhemann

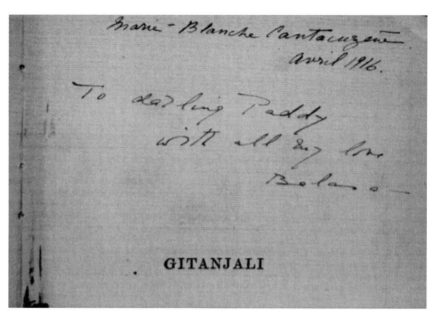

Inscription to Paddy in Gitanjali, a collection of poems by Rabindranath Tagore
[V.A.Urechia Library, Galați]

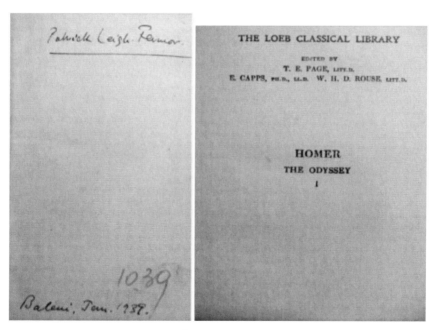

Paddy's Homer [V.A.Urechia Library, Galați]

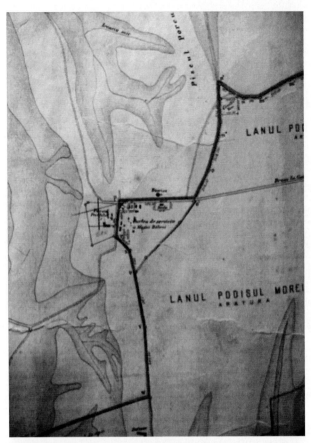

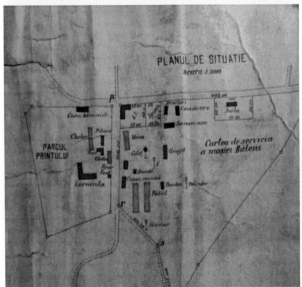

The Băleni Estate 1903

PART 3
1946-1965

Nicolae Ceauşescu, 'the Genius of the Carpathians', and friends 1966

In October 1947, a fragment of poem by Balaşa reached Paddy[1]:

> *'I have come back, worn with fatigue, and lonely,*
> *From a sad world that sinks in utter void.*
> *I have come back, Băleni , wise and there*
> *For us that suffer, and our heart and bleed*
> *I was once remembered;*
> *But who remembers save you and me,*
> *the smell of moonlit lilies*
> *Then all the paths seemed open for my taking!'* [2]

---

[1] NLS Acc.13338/129.

[2] Paddy thought this may have been written after the 1940 earthquake.

Chapter Seven

THE CURTAIN FALLS

The Red Army arrives in Bucharest

Back in Athens at the end of the war, this time as a 30-year-old highly decorated former Lieutenant Colonel in the Intelligence Corps and Deputy Director of the British Institute of Higher English Studies [British Council], Paddy received a letter from Balaşa on 27 January 1946 [1]. 'Paddy darling, I heard you are in Athens…When you rode on Băleni fields and swished at the maize stalks shouting "Mountjoie St Denis"[2] you were preparing your life'.

She goes on to recall the circumstances of their parting. 'I am glad that when we heard on the wireless in the car by The Balta[3] that war was declared and we all packed yours and Henry Neville's things and dashed with you to Bucharest and Eileen and I saw you off on that first train on 7th September that neither she nor I said a word to keep you a bit longer…as your heart and soul were straining for it. Paddy, these years have been messy, long and awful'.

---

[1] ibid.

[2] The war-cry of the French Knights.

[3] Pond or lake.

After recounting how she never heard any news of him during the war, she explains how she knew he was alive. '..I knew it already by a dream and I dream seldom – you were sitting at the foot of my bed in the dream, and we were talking, and I said: "Talk to me about Guy" and you turned your face to the window and said something, then you said: "Guy has been dead so long[4]" and then I woke – it was in the middle of the night in August 1940[5] – and I cried for hours, and thought of you both and wondered what it meant but I felt that Guy had left us.

Paddy, I know nothing about you except your glorious past in the war. I hope you have kept your heart and soul alive as ever and I don't doubt you have. I hope also that you have been happy, now and then and for the future. You have such a wonderful kinship with human beings that you must have met wonderful people that you brought out on your way – I always wondered how you could get in touch with the best…every time you met a person. It is a gift.

After six years and more since we last saw each other darling I still feel I can write to you as if I was speaking to you and it is so lovely – I think it will always be so – you gave me those perfect years of your beautiful young life – we probably learnt a lot from each other. At any rate I am deeply grateful for them and I hope you may not feel they were wasted. You were so generous darling in the gift of your lovely mind and heart and taught one so many things. I had new outlooks and understanding of things through your broad and kind way of meeting people and circumstances. I shall never forget, Paddy, what you meant to me and I have kept for you everything that will be yours forever.'

One thing Balaşa did not know was that Paddy had found a new soul mate and lover in Joan Rayner née Eyres Monsell. They had met in Cairo shortly after Christmas 1944 and when they returned to England the following summer, Joan had taken Paddy to stay at Dumbleton Hall, her spacious family home in Worcestershire. Their paths crossed again in Athens that November and they had travelled together to Salonika and then, with Paddy's wartime friend Xan Fielding, to Rhodes where they stayed with Larry Durrell and his lover Eve Cohen. Much closer to Paddy in age – she was just three years older – artistic, intelligent and well connected, Joan was totally smitten by the new man in her life. On his part, Paddy was equally 'head over heels' but never at the expense of his freedom to do whatever or go wherever he pleased.

---

[4] Aged 27, Guy was killed in action flying his Hurricane fighter over the English Channel on 11 August 1940.

[5] Pru Branch had kept in touch with Balaşa . In 1940, she sent her a book of Garcia Lorca's poetry.

Escaping from the mêlée of Athenian streets on the Easter weekend of 1946, Paddy set off for Poros, determined to reply to Balaşa's latest letter to him. '[Saturday] The clock has suddenly slipped back the years, and here I am sitting in front of our café in the small square[6], at a green topped iron table in one of those rickety chairs…[Sunday] Darling, I am again at the café, quiet, happy, sun-drenched and am filled with the most terrific 'love' for you. Yesterday I got Yanni to row me to the bay of Artemis and lay in the sun all afternoon, watching the shadow change on the island. Towards dusk, I shook myself and walked through the wood where the white horse used to gallop aimlessly and I used to talk of half-submerged trunks [?]. Then through that sloping golden glade to the minute church, the narrow path till the place where the donkey used to pace round and round, drawing up the water, and up through the lemon groves, to the mill. My darling, it was a moment I had been aching for, and, of course, dreading, for the last six years but, Boodle, there it was, as if nothing had changed. I stood and watched through the branches: Marina busy at the oven, Spiro, cheeks puffed with feigned and endearing exertion, emptying lemons into huge barrel. [After lunch on the return journey to Poros] I dived overboard and swam for a while in the cold sea on the way back and now sit at the old table with the caïque masts thick in front, the salt flaking on my new burnt arms, the sunlight still warm in my dilated limbs and arms. This is where I wrote that first sonnet when you went to Athens and I almost feel that tomorrow I will see you walking down the gangway…in your grey wool Athens suit, silk shirt, blue and white tie, and small round white hat.'

His letter[7] was never posted.

Stranded in Bucharest in post-war Romania, Balaşa continued to correspond to her 'Nutkin'. By now she knew about Joan and on 1 July 1947 she wrote[8]: 'I love to think of Joan and you – she sounds lovely. Don't lose each other – happiness is just two roads crossing, two persons understanding each other. Do you remember when you said to me once, when we first met each other: "You will not cage me, will you?" "Did I?" We were happy for those four years before the war – then you left and were free as a sea gull. My sweet, I have nothing but gratitude towards you and think of you as the purest loveliest person I have ever known'.

---

[6] In Galatas, the nearest town to Lemonodassos.

[7] NLS Acc.13338/134.

[8] NLS Acc.13338/129.

Then on 25 August 1947, Bill Bentinck[9] received a letter from Balaşa with grim news: 'It's all over. A[lexandru] and I have been in prison for two weeks which seemed endless'. It transpired that with the spectre of a Stalinist government looming larger by the day, Alexandru Moruzi and Balaşa had decided it was time to flee to the West. They made their way to the busy port of Constanţa on the Black Sea and, with the help of Lieutenant-Commander Zama from the Port Administration and M. Ionescu, a retired captain and the owner of a mechanical repair shop, set about organizing their escape. A key member of the team was Nicolae Udrea, an agricultural machinery mechanic who had worked on the estate at Băleni. Alexandru gave him 200 million lei to find a hull of a small vessel 'for dolphin fishing in the waters off Sulina[10]. Their real destination was of course Istanbul and from there to Greece. Presumably this ploy was to avoid the attention of the authorities who were on the look-out for purchases of seaworthy vessels. More money went on obtaining sailing permits alongside other costs like navigation lamps, lifejackets, large salvage coils, gasoline, and most importantly a heavy-duty engine.

Waiting for the installation of the engine and then the sea trials, Balaşa and Alexandru opted to spend the rest of the summer in a villa in the quiet seaside village of Costineşti, a few miles south of Constanţa. Nearby, another group of fugitives – Dan Pleşia, Petre Mironescu, Ion Dendrino, Nicolae Krupenski and Nicolae Racottă[11] – who, having secretly congregated at the Villa Berindei, were busy planning their own clandestine flight to Istanbul. Their security was poor and when the gendarmerie made the first arrests at Villa Berindei, Balaşa and Alexandru managed to slip away and went into hiding in Udrea's house in Constanţa. Two days later, they too were arrested. It turned out that, from the very start, Udrea had been a communist informer and accused them of involving him in 'a Manist plot'[12].

In hindsight, both were lucky that a modicum of the rule of law still applied and the charge of attempted escape could not be proven in spite of the fact that Alexandru had 250 million Lei on him and an expensive set of binoculars. Their interrogators also tracked down a large suitcase they

---

[9] He kept in touch with Balaşa throughout her life, sending her books and money.

[10] A port at the mouth of the Sulina tributary of the Danube delta.

[11] In 1944, Racottă's brother had escaped to Egypt with the industrialist Max Auşnit in a light plane flown by Matei Ghika.

[12] Paul Păltânea and Mihai Dim. Sturdza: *Istoria Moşiei Băleni din Ţinutul Covurlui.*

had left with Ilinca Florescu in Bucharest but fortunately failed to make the connection that she was the sister of the recently arrested Baron Ionel Mocsonyi-Stârcea. A year later, the consequences would have been much direr. George Cantacuzino, the architect whose wife and children were in England, had attempted a similar escape from Constanța. Discovered at the last minute, he had made his way over the adjoining rooftops and walked almost a 100 miles to the Bibescu house at Posada where, recognized by the servants, he found refuge in the loft. He was betrayed to the security services by the local cobbler who had been asked to repair his worn-out shoes. Hidden in the hay stacked in the attic, he gave himself up as the police methodically stabbed each stook with pitchforks. Unlike Balașa and Alexandru, he was sentenced to 5 years imprisonment, branded an enemy of the people and never allowed to leave Romania. Such was the punishment for being born a Prince irrespective of his superlative contribution to Romanian architecture and courageous wartime service as an official war artist.

At the end of September, Balașa returned to Băleni and wrote to Paddy[13] that: 'this place is really a house for Tired Souls. I am writing at the round stone table where we have dined so often. The afternoon light is slanting under the fir trees that are left. I can see the hills from where I sit and they look like a dark sea. All the alleys at the bottom of the garden have disappeared…the house looks astonishingly young in its whiteness and green shutters…You are part of Băleni, Paddy, and when at night I pass through the rooms to the library you are there with a light looking for a book with a pile of books on the floor that you are sorting. The books are still here.'[14]

Ever since Decree 187 of 23 March 1945 when the Communists announced their land reforms, anyone owning over 50 hectares came under intense pressure from local Communist activists. The Donicis were no exception; the grain harvest at Băleni was blocked and Pomme had had to go to court to recover 21 hectares which had been illegally expropriated[15]. Although they were under no illusions of the severity of the fate that lay in store for them, the sisters and Constantin clung to the Tolstoyan ideal that even if everything was confiscated, they would somehow be allowed to work on the land side by side with the peasants. They waited for 1949 in trepidation. Balașa wrote to Paddy describing how she was living in 'Fifi's

---

[13] NLS Acc.13338/ Letter 28 September 1947.

[14] Paul Păltânea and Mihai Dim. Sturdza: *Istoria Moșiei Băleni din Ținutul Covurlui.*

[15] Dorin and Mariana Pintilie: *Comuna Băleni: Studiu monographic complex*, Editura Eurodidact, Cluj, 2003.

the housekeeper's room so that the rest of the house is closed in order to deter vagabonds'. In a desperate sign off, she exclaimed 'Oh Paddy, when shall I accomplish my dream and have a little house on a Greek island?'[16]

On the night of 2/3 March 1949, a group of Communist activists forced their way into the manor house at Băleni and demanded with menace that the Cantacuzino sisters and Constantin Donici signed a document 'donating' the land and the house to the state. They were powerless to resist but collective memory recalls 'fear in their eyes and the trembling of their hands'[17]. Having signed, they were peremptorily ordered to dress in heavy clothing and to put whatever necessities they needed in a small suitcase. They were given fifteen minutes. On the outskirts of the village, an open lorry waited in the snow. The activists herded Constantin and the sisters into the back where they found Gogu Vasiliu[18], the estate manager, and Racovița already on board. With no tarpaulin to protect them from the snow, they were driven thirty miles to the station in Galați. A local person who witnessed their arrival, remembered 'it was so cold that the snow itself shivered. Princesses Elena and Balaşa , Donici, Vasilui, Racovița – I saw all of them. Each one of them had a small suitcase. They loaded them in cattle trucks, probably to scatter them throughout the country'.

As Paddy later put it, 'a sudden Dark Age descended that nobody was ready for'.[19]

Their journey ended in an attic studio at Pucioasa, a large farming village[20] on the southern slopes of the Carpathians to the west of Bucharest where they were initially forced to earn a living as employees of the town's waste collection service. In 1951, they are shown registered at 18 Strada Libertăţii, a cruel irony given the lack of liberty that marked their existence at that time. Balaşa reportedly managed to retain her Bohemian nature, continuing to paint and to dress in a bizarre fashion, and Pomme became a teacher at School No.4[21]. Communications with the outside world were difficult but not impossible for in 1961 Balaşa wrote a long letter to Paul Sân-Petru discussing the work of the Nobel prize-winning

---

[16] NLS Acc.13338/129.

[17] ibid.

[18] Vasilui had been warned: he was patiently waiting with his suitcase when the activists arrived at his house.

[19] Letter PLF to Marie-Lyse Ruhemann.

[20] In 1948, its population was 4, 643.

[21] A memorial head and shoulders sculpture of her was unveiled at the school in 2017.

French poet, Saint-John Perse.[22] However, apart from this fragment, there is virtually no written or hearsay evidence of their life in the '50s and early '60s until 1965 when Paddy suddenly resurfaced in Romania.

---

[22] Letter Balaşa Cantacuzino to Paul San-Petru [V.A.Urechia library].

Chapter Eight

TOUTES LES TRISTESSES DU MONDE

The Party on the march, Pucioasa 1947

It was in Pucioasa that Balaşa and Paddy were reunited in June 1965, 26 years after their wartime separation. Using his cover as a journalist on assignment for *Holiday Magazine*, Paddy tells how he arranged to meet Ina Donici in Bucharest who spirited him away to Pucioasa at night on the back of a borrowed motorbike[1]. After 48 hours closeted with the two sisters in their tiny flat, he returned to Bucharest with Ina. He wrote to Joan 'I'm so pleased I went: it was a momentous thing for everyone concerned. I haven't quite come round from it yet, half marvellous, half terribly sad and shattering'. By all accounts, the 66-year-old Balaşa was 'a broken ruin' of her former self.

There are some odd aspects to Paddy's account of this visit. When Ina

---

[1] Artemis Cooper: Patrick Leigh Fermor, an Adventure.

heard from Balaşa[2] that he was thinking about coming to Romania as part of his Danube writing assignment, she wrote to Paddy: 'Throughout all these years you never seemed really remote…I feel it will be quite natural for you to materialize out of thin air one morning, quite unchanged I am sure and full of all the charm and fun one remembers so well. In the way of sight-seeing, I can offer you a tour around the country on our motorbike which I drive quite well and not on the wrong side of the highroad as you seem to do with cars'[3].

Then, in the *Daily Telegraph* article of 12 May 1990, Paddy says that 'the pre-war company I had kept had put me on a blacklist; for good, it seemed… The moment the veto was lifted I went back to Romania in 1965, with a short-term visa'. If this was the case, one would expect to find a Siguranta/Securitate file on him but there does not appear to be one[4]. Contrast this to the experience of Eric Tappe, a member of the British Military Mission 1944–46 in Romania, who had been advised by the FO not to attempt to travel to Romania until 1964. His Securitate file during his visit reveals that he was shadowed everywhere. Roy MacGregor-Hastie who arrived in Bucharest in 1957 for Express Newspapers, found that he had two 'keepers'. Tudor 'the neurologist' kept tabs on him during the day and Doina, 'a beautiful girl with long black hair' shared his bed at night[5]. Paddy's innocuous pre-war status in Romania would not have qualified him for such attention by the state.

In the same article, no mention is made of *Holiday Magazine* which had commissioned him to write an article about travelling down the Danube from its source to the Black Sea, a route that would take him past Romania[6]. In 1965, a foreign journalist would normally have had a State Security 'minder' whose job was to watch over his charge and report on his moments. However, given that the nature of his assignment was to promote tourism, Paddy would have most likely been exempt from such close scrutiny.

Nevertheless, he still flags up that he was putting the sisters and Ina at considerable risk. 'Mixing with foreigners incurred severe punishment, but harbouring them indoors was much worse; so the visit had to be made by stealth, at night, and on the back of a motorbike borrowed by the Orphelia

---

[2] NLS Acc.13338/134 Letter PLF to Balaşa Cantacuzino 20 April 1965.

[3] NLS Acc.13338/19.

[4] National Centre for the Study of Securitate Archives.

[5] Roy MacGregor-Hastie: Don't send me to Omsk!, Macdonald, 1961.

[6] Published in August 1966.

niece, who was working as a draughtswoman in Bucharest'[7]. Indeed any such contact was a notifiable offence. So why put them in jeopardy? The answer probably lies in the fact that police surveillance of Balaşa and the Donicis had been lifted in 1963 and they were no longer persons of interest to the authorities[8]. This had been communicated to Paddy who nevertheless chose to embroider his journey as another SOE escapade!

However, the actual 100-kilometre journey to Pucioasa would have been extremely risky in itself. Driving at night in Romania was notoriously difficult at that time for Russian-made lorries and buses did not have dip switches. Their drivers were therefore left with no choice other than to turn their headlights off as they approached one another from the opposite direction. In the ensuing pitch darkness, collisions were frequent.

Balaşa was overjoyed, writing to Paddy on 5 June that 'it was marvellous to find you so unchanged after 26 years of separation'. Likewise, Ina was thrilled by the visit – 'It has made us all so happy, like beneficent rain after a drought'[9]. And there was, for her, a surprising twist for the day after Paddy left, she and her husband, Michael Catargi, were notified to get their papers ready to leave for France. The motorbike was left in Pucioasa and sold.

It was the first of several reunions and many long joyous letters followed and consignments of books despatched from John Sandoe on Paddy's account[10]. Pomme and Ina visited Kardamyli twice in the 1970s but 'B couldn't make it alas!...I wish she had and stayed out'. There were great plans, but bad health, among other things, intervened. Ina got away to Paris, where she and Michael, a brilliant linguist, worked as translators. At one point, they were offered a two-year contract to work for the French Ministry of Foreign Affairs in Niamey in Niger but ill-health intervened and they never went.

Paddy had made a great impression on the young Ina when he lived at Băleni. Once contact had been resumed, she wrote regularly to him in a style he certainly would have approved of. 'For Paddy. This bit of ancient silver, dug out of the deep rich soil of the Râpa Roşie – that valley by our vineyard where always at this time of year red poppies came out of the grass over the bones of warriors slain there 400 years ago, fighting the dreaded Turkish armies.'

---

[7] In *Words of Mercury*, he writes: 'Mixing with foreigners incurred severe punishment, but harbouring them indoors was much worse'.

[8] Correspondence author and Prof Denis Deletant, June 2017.

[9] NLS Acc.13338/19 Letter Ina to PLF dated 20 June 1965.

[10] NLS Acc.13338/ 129–134 Letter PLF to Balaşa Cantacuzino 15 November 1965.

In another letter, she asks: 'do you remember the road over the hill, which one always looked at from the library in Băleni, winding up in a single, perfectly beautiful coil, like a shell growing, sand white between the yellow clay cliffs, then disappearing in a sudden turn over the edge – the symbol, as one felt the mood appropriate, of the unobtainable outside world, or, on the contrary, of voyages planned and entered into with all the spirit of adventure and discovery and creative passion.' Ina died of breast cancer in Paris in 1981.

On 7 January 1976, when Balaşa was recovering from an operation, Pomme wrote to Paddy and Joan with their news[11]. Half way through the letter, Balaşa, who was too weak to write, interjected with this dictation: 'My dear ones, when my heart is very bad I always want Paddy to know this that I never told him. We were coming back by moonlight to the mill [at Lemonodassos]. Paddy had gone on in front and I could hear him singing lustily "Raggle Taggle Gypsies Oh!" among the lemon groves. I had lagged behind and sat on a little stone wall. I felt at that moment that I had never been happier than before and would never be happier – Bless his heart'.

Balaşa died on 11 March 1976 in great pain with her beloved sister Pomme at her bedside. She decided to send both the ashes of her husband Constantin Donici, who had died nine years previously, and her sister's body to be laid to rest in the family crypt at Băleni. One of her former pupils, a young engineer, loaded Balaşa's coffin on top of his car and drove it 200 miles to Băleni. Villagers from far and wide came to pay their respects to Balaşa, who, dressed in a light coloured flowery summer dress, lay in an open coffin. Now the earth of the village which she could never give up received her.[12]

Distraught at the loss of her sister, Pomme wrote to Paddy 'her last thought was for you two and for Alexandre – those who had been closest and written to her most often during the last months of her illness. Your letters were her one joy. The tie with her past and the places she had been to and loved. She started a letter when her right hand was a little better after the operation but could only write the first three words, "My dear Ones"'.

Derek Patmore fondly wrote that she 'inspired love and returned it and deep and lasting friendships were the mainstay of her life'. In a life that

---

[11] NLS Acc.13338/ 129–134 Letter PLF to Balaşa Cantacuzino 15 November 1965.

[12] Dorin and Mariana Pintilie: *Comuna Băleni – Studiu monographic complex*, Editura Eurodidact, Cluj, 2003.

had witnessed violent and destructive change, the years at Băleni remained her most precious memory for here was the living theatre which she had created. In the time between her divorce and the beginning of war, Balaşa designed the set, chose the actors and then let their voices speak and the laughter flow. In a poem, written in French and called *Anniversaire 2 Mars*, she returns to Băleni, the 'custodian of my secret thoughts':

Hey, you airy rooms, tonight I listen to your silence
And, like a ghost, open your doors without so much as a noise
Only to rediscover over those many years the rhythm
And the span of days and nights gone by.

Just as in those long skids of childhood
Along your polished and creaking floors,
That ancient edifice welcomes the nomad
And smiles sadly at her game.
Persian tapestries depicting trudging elephants
Still hang from its walls and
In the vases white flowers plucked long ago
Slowly die.

That chess game still lies on the table
By the large fireplace
Which drew in all our tales
And transformed them into smoke.

The mirrors reflect the many faces
Which stared into them over the years.
Dogs bark far away in the village
Whilst the large owl flying by
Issues its plaintive cry; an omen
Which none of us wanted to hear.

Uneased, I halt at the threshold of my bedroom
Where the draft blows through the cracks in the wall
And a wisteria branch which flowers at all seasons
Has sinewed itself into the shadows.

Looming towards me like a caravel
I see my large blue canopied bed
Floating on the wooden floor like a palanquin.
Frescoes in a joyous array of rainbows triumph over fissures
To reveal transposed gardens and floral arabesques.

All around me are the shadows of my modest offerings
To this world in chosen moments of solitude and darkness.
At the dead of sleepless nights I stealthily step away from these ruins,
Custodian of my secret thoughts, and dance before the mirror
In a magical process of transformation.

Squealing shutters conjure up snow squalls and summer storms,
Dust which used to come in through gaps in old windows, badly shut.
Slowly I go through the doors of this unfathomable past
And lose myself in the twilight of those abandoned alleys.

[Translated: Geoffrey Cardozo]

Paddy's love affair with Balaşa remained in the long evening shadows of their private intimacy. Passing references in *Words of Mercury*, an article in the *Daily Telegraph Weekend Magazine* of May 1990 and the introduction to *The World Mine Oyster* only provide a brief peek into their four years together before war broke out. We are merely told that 'a light hearted affinity sprang up' between Paddy and Balaşa, 'one of the two sisters who were our hostesses' at Băleni'. Maybe that is how they both wanted their affair to be remembered as they were propelled into the unfurling storm of war.

In a letter to Marie-Lise Cantacuzino many years later[13], Paddy wrote 'how I wished that Balaşa, when told to pack at Băleni – one suitcase only, and in quarter of an hour, by the people in the Securitate truck – as well as finding my own voluminous notebook, on which everything I'm writing is based, had happened to remember her own memoirs. She was putting them together all through the year before the war, especially in winter 1938–39. She wrote beautifully and, if saved, it would have been a marvellous record. There were lots of memories of her grandfather, the 'Kniaz', and all the stories she had heard from the last two or three generations. Very interesting, very moving sometimes and often funny.'

---

[13] Letter PLF to Marie-Lyse Ruhemann 10 January 1994.

PART 4
1966–2017

Bucharest 1989

HUNTING

I've never run after words.
All I have sought
Was their long
Silvery shadows,
Dragged by the sun through the grass,
Or drawn by the moon over the sea;
I've never hunted anything
But the words' shadows –
It is very skilful hunting
Learned from old folks
Who know
That there's nothing more precious
About a word
Than its shadow
And devoid of their shadows
Are the words that have sold their souls.

Ana Blandiana, Founder member of the Romanian
Civic Alliance. Translated by Dan Duțescu

Chapter Nine

ROMANIA REVISITED

Of the conac, nothing remains, all traces of the Cantacuzino Princely Court having been systematically eradicated.

The characters that went on to play such memorable parts in *Between the Woods and the Water* continued to haunt Paddy. '…When war broke out, all these friends vanished into sudden darkness. Afterwards the uprooting and destruction were on so tremendous a scale that it was sometimes years after the end of it all that the cloud became less dense and I could pick up a clue here and there and piece together what had happened in the interim. Nearly all of them had been dragged into the conflict in the teeth of their true feelings and disaster overtook them all'[1].

In March 1987, Rudi Fischer tracked Xenia Csernovics down through her nephew Miklós Vajda and located her in Budapest[2]. After the war, as a class enemy, she had been sent to do menial work as a house painter and later to work in a textile factory in Budapest. She ended her days in a basement flat which she moved to after she strangled her former flatmate

---

[1] *Between the Woods and the Water*, Chapter 5.

[2] NLS Acc.13338/44 and 45.

in a fit of rage in Pannonia Street on 20 December 1969. Such was her popularity with her neighbours that many of them testified in court to the justification of her actions, claiming that the victim was an unbearable woman, thus leading to a reduced charge of manslaughter[3].

Letters were exchanged, with Xenia addressing Paddy as 'Dear Michael', the name he had been called in those early pre-war days. 'I think very often of Zam when I was a little girl. Happy years as a young girl with my dogs and horses…This life is forever finished, no chateaux, no happy life.' Although Xenia struck a note of wistfulness and sadness in all her letters, she filled them with news of her daughter Mária Teleki and rejoiced in the company of a pigeon which she had adopted after finding it hobbling around with a bandaged foot. With the pigeon looking on, she wrote 'I never will forget your séjour at Zam' and reminded him of Aunt Margot who 'came to see us one afternoon. Do you remember? And she found your slips on my toilette table. She told Jenő Teleki'[4]. In his 1990 Romanian notebook, Paddy remembered Zam 'as a setting for outdoor feasts and midnight bathes'. Xenia died in 1990.

Elemér Klobusiczky had reappeared earlier in Paddy's life when contact was made between the two of them in 1975. Married with two daughters, he was living in Budapest and making a living as a translator. In a letter to Rudi Fischer of 7 July 1978[5], Paddy tells of meeting him in Budapest, living as a translator of scientific documents. 'I drove with him and his sister Ilona and a nice ex-sculptress called Mrs Strasser to Esztergom and Visegrad spending hours looking at pictures in the palace[6] I hadn't seen for half a century.' Elemér, who died in 1986, wrote to Paddy in 1981 with news of some of the other actors. 'Klara Zelinski is somewhere in Poland. Her husband died long ago'. And 'as for old Woracziczky [née Kintzig] and her "Jankovits", I know the following: she burned in her bed, dead drunk, after she overturned her oil lamp. Jankovits, who was a very elegant Hussar officer, was found on the [illegible] also drunk, frozen to death. He had not a penny and in his pocket there was a legitimentation[7] issued for beggars.'

Alexandru Moruzi, who had played the role of a devoted brother to Balaşa, had escaped to Switzerland where he lived with his menagerie

---

[3] https://patrickleighfermor.org/tag/budapest/

[4] NLS Acc.13338/33.

[5] NLS Acc.13338/44.

[6] He must be referring to the Keresztény Múzeum which is housed in the Primate's Palace in Esztergom.

[7] Government permit.

of cats and painted furiously for six hours every day. Of his work, little is known other than the twenty-two card designs in *Le Tarot Mystique* published in 1983. On reading *Between the Woods and the Water*, he wrote to Paddy in January 1987 that 'the old man I have become felt suddenly younger and strong, intoxicated by the rich flavours of the unknown destiny that was still in front of us'[8].

In March 1982, Paddy decided he needed to revisit Hungary and Romania[9], not least to refresh his memory as he made final edits to the manuscript of *Between the Woods and the Water*. In Budapest he took his old friend Elemér out to lunch and then flew to Bucharest. Sitting in Capşa Restaurant on the Calea Victoriei, he wrote in his notebook 'the last time I was in this room was in September 1939. I'm at the same table, as far as I can guess, as I was then – with Balaşa, Pomme, Constantin, Matila and Eileen Ghika and Henry Nevile. A few yards away sat Nicky Chrissoloveni with Ursula Howard-Stepney[10]'. He goes on to list Cholmeley, Antoine and Elizabeth Bibesco[11], and young Priscilla Bibesco, 'wide-eyed, chin lifted like a waterbird of a particularly nice kind'. After hiring a car, he drove up to Pucioasa to spend time with Pomme, who by now was living on her own.

He now embarked on a journey that retraced the route he had taken in 1934, starting at Baron Tibor's house at Mocrea where he 'tried to spot the window of the room where love making took place. Thought of Rita and Tibor[12], and games, funny stories'. The reality was that the house had become a state mental institution. Passing through Maria Radna, he overshot Mr von Konopy's house and had to go back to Odvoş, an experience he later wove into the book. To his surprise, he found the inhabitants of Căpâlnaş were also 'now loonies' and noted that Count Jenő had died there in 1947. According to the Medical Officer he met there, Countess Tinka 'had been sent off with a State Licence to beg'. Tinka and her family had become the targets of a vicious class war in which the objective of the Communists was to eradicate the power and influence of the aristocracy, irrespective of their individual merits and qualifications. Although Tinka and Bubi were allowed to remain in the house after 1948, their status was that of 'forced residents'. 'Bubi' Teleki was later arrested and tortured in

---

[8] NLS Acc.13338/83.

[9] NLS Acc.13338/524.

[10] Her father, Sir James Horlick Bt, had served with distinction in Greece in the First World War and had become a friend of the King and Queen of Greece.

[11] She was the daughter of Herbert Asquith, British Prime Minister [1908–16].

[12] Baron Tibor died in 1948.

prison. On release, he found a menial job on the railway and became an alcoholic. He died on 25 August 1980 at Geoagiu in Hunedoara County, a town on the Mureş to the east of Deva. Count Jenő's priceless collection of moths and the contents of his extensive library were destroyed when the house became a TB sanatorium for children.

At Zam, 'another loony bin', Paddy met 'an old geezer' who remembered tales of the Csernovits family – the old father and 'above all, dear Xenia'. Mysteriously he refers to 'talk of Gábor's suicide' but 'no mention of the murder'. Both Xenia's husband and son were called Gábor and both died in 1945. Down the road, he raised a glass of excellent Klobusiczky tuica to Elemér's health with the new occupants of Gurasada which had become an experimental bamboo farm.

At this stage, Paddy collected his thoughts about the fictional Transylvanian journey with 'Angela' and Elemér for he needed more material to anchor it. In rapid succession, he visited Deva, Alba Julia [a fine Gothic cathedral 'shut of course' and a Maria Theresa gateway], Cluj [The Hotel Continental], Turda, Târgu Mureş, Sighişoara ['a wooden covered staircase', 'a place of great magic'] and Făgăraş. As to what he gleaned, there is but a smidgeon recorded in his notebook: it was undoubtedly a rushed journey with little time to linger and observe.

Eight years later, in February 1990, *The Daily Telegraph* commissioned Paddy to write a piece on post-Ceauşescu Romania. Alec Russell, a young stringer for the newspaper, was detailed by the foreign editor to tend to his needs. Russell recalls that 'profoundly depressed by the legacy of communism on the Romania he had known and loved in the thirties, Paddy returned from visits to his old friends full of regrets about happier times. But, with an unimpaired appetite for tuiça and late-night conversation, he made a fascinating travel companion, briefly raising the veil from an earlier and more glorious Balkan age'[13].

It was an ambitious brief for it was only a few weeks since the dramatic events of Christmas Eve 1989 and the summary execution of Nicolai and Elena Ceauşescu. He flew to a still shell-shocked Timişoara with Russell and then with Clare Arron, *The Daily Telegraph*'s photographer, at the wheel of a hired car, he headed for Oradea, passing Ineu en route, and from there to Sighet, before crossing the Eastern Carpathians into the Bucovina.

'Soon we were following pebbly river beds under steep beechwoods from one Byzantine monastery to another, with Chaucerian nuns in robes and black pill-boxes murmuring explanations of the mural paintings;

---

[13] Alec Russell: *Prejudice and Plum Brandy*, Michael Joseph 1993.

smoking russet and orange and lapis lazuli Trees of Jesse, Martyrdoms, Transfigurations and Sieges of Constantinople which were frescoed all over the church walls inside and out. It was in between two of these monasteries – Moldoviţa, by its rushing brooks, and the great woodland fortress of Suceviţa – that snow began falling again, turning the forest passes into a dim world of white feathers and whirling specks. In slow motion the wheels of the car slid on the newly covered ice, skewed off the road and into a ditch, a front wheel mercifully disabled by striking the ramp of a bridge. As it grew darker, we toyed dramatically with thoughts of battening down for the night while wolves eyes shone through the dark and crowd the window panes…'[14].

At one stage, he visited Băleni which had vanished. 'Some forbidding industrial buildings, already old and battered, [were] in its place and the trees had all been cut down'. What a wretched sight it must have been for him. The article appeared as *Rumania–Travels in a Land before Darkness Fell* in the *Daily Telegraph Weekend Magazine* of 12 May 1990.

And what of the houses today?

The Solymossy kastély at Mocrea continues as the Spital de Psihiatrie Mocrea, 'a hulking custard yellow building at the end of an avenue of trees' where Nick Hunt looked in as he followed Paddy's footsteps through Romania in 2012.[15] Here, he found an interior of 'over-lit, disinfected corridors' with 'compulsively smoking characters shuffling between the rooms'. No trace remained of its previous incarnation and no nuggets of collective memory about its once noble owners were proffered. Little had changed in 2017 and when asked whether it was possible to visit, the guard on the gate replied 'only if you have a severe mental condition'. The surrounding vineyards are still much in evidence as is the hill of Mokra which rises high to the East of the kastély, a solitary outpost of the blue grey Zalanti Massif which heralds the borderland of Transylvania and the start of the Apuseni Mountains. It was here on its summit that the midnight feast took place, a bonfire lit and a Gypsy band assembled.

The low ranch-like white manor house of Jas and Klara Zelensky does indeed still stand 'among cornfields under a clump of elms', not at Tövisegyháza but by the side of the Curtuci – Sântana road on the eastern extremity of the *puszta*, the Great Hungarian Plain. Speckled with blots

---

[14] NLS Acc.13339/528 and 529.

[15] *Walking the Woods and the Water.*

of herded sheep moving slowly along in woolly huddled ranks, the fields around the house stretch to the horizon and beyond. Now hidden in a dense jungle of poplars and acacias, its pale green shutters cling to the window frames like survivors holding on to a life raft. Ceiling have collapsed and the musty stench of rotting wood mixed with dust and mold is all pervasive.

Paddy wrote that the Kintzigs reputedly died in a fire in 'the combustible manor house'. Although both Georgette and her mother both died in 1945, the manor house at Scanteia/Tövisegyháza never burnt down. It is now run as the Hotel Domeniul Lupaş, a flourishing business specializing in wedding receptions. Sadly, although he remembers 'every detail of this house…and the inhabitants, the servants, the dogs and horses and the scenery…', Paddy offers no description of either the exterior or interior of Kintzig kastély, which are both a testament of Art Nouveau and Secessionist design. Everywhere there are curves to give shape to the square forms, windows are surmounted by ornate stonework hoods with motifs of bristling thistles and clad with guards of intricate wrought iron tracery outlining giant flowers. Balconies boast roundel apertures and the canopy over the entrance is supported by two thin iron columns protruding from plump marble stanchions. Inside the house, above doors inset with stained glass, there is a plethora of floral decoration embedded in friezes on ceilings supported by polished faux braces and embossed on walls. The resplendent bulbous cheeks of the great pink marble fire place in the main hall exhale slowly as they taper to form the double helmeted mantle. Compared to some of the more extravagant and fantastic Secessionist buildings, Tövisegyháza is a modest example but in its day it must have made a startling impression in the rusticity of the Partium.

Paddy's 'high Baroque pile', the Franciscan Abbey of Maria Radna, continues to welcome elderly pilgrims who appeared out of the autumn mist by coachloads. Beckoned by the bells, each clutching a crucifix of the Saviour, they wended their way up the slope towards the twin cupolas.

Two recent travel writers have followed Paddy to Căpâlnaş. Tom Fort in *Against the Flow: Wading through Eastern Europe* [2010] tracked down 82-year-old Countess Gemma Teleki, who ran a flower stall outside the gates of the Teleki Library in Târgu Mureş. This inspired him to explore the Mureş valley where he visited the kastélys at Căpâlnaş and Zam, both psychiatric hospitals in the early 1990s. In 2011, Nick Hunt began his own 'great trudge' on foot to Istanbul and, like Paddy, he crossed the border into Romania at Curtici. He too met up with a Teleki, this time Ileana, the great-granddaughter of Count Jenő Teleki, Paddy's host at Căpâlnaş. The two of them made a tour – 'a trail of ruins' – of Căpâlnaş, Odvoş and

Bulci, the last two being in a state of forlorn disrepair. He found Count Jenő's 'grave in the woods'.

Although a Spitalul de Psihiatrie like Mocrea, Căpâlnaş, a neat and tidy boxlike petit Trianon, has evaded the strictures of institutionalization for externally it is, to all extants, identical to the house that Paddy stayed in. Deep in 'the dense woods [that] shot up steeply behind the house' are the graves of Count Jenő and his little daughter Mady, marked by two ranks of small stone columns that stand solemnly like guards around a catafalque in a towering cathedral of beech trees with a vaulted ceiling of intertwined branches. The same stillness and quiet prevailed except for the intermittent raucous solo of a jay or the silent glide of an eagle owl descending from its perch.

Close by, the kastély at Bulci, once the hub of intrigue and Royalist plots, is fast losing its battle with nature which has reclaimed the once perfectly manicured gardens and lawns at a fearsome pace. Secondary growth now obscures all but the most trodden paths which are little more than animal tracks. Still trapped in the dead hand of state ownership, the deserted house mourns for days of former glory; tears of ivy stream down its façade blotched with rampant veins of ruddy creeper.

Kastély Odvoş lies forlornly awaiting a buyer. Hovering on the brink of ruination, bombarded by the vibrations of juggernauts thundering along the East-West arterial road just yards from its ochre-coloured façade, this Neo-Classical gem of a manor house has been long abandoned and left to die of dereliction. Behind it stands the 18th century family church, a study in perfect proportion, in a state of collapse and terminal strangulation by the encroaching undergrowth. On the south wall there is a slate-coloured rectangular stone slab with an embossed crucifix and a garland of corn draped across the upright. Below, a plaque supported by sheaves of wheat on either side bears the simple inscription 'Konopi Kalman, 21 January 1880 – 26 November 1947'.

There is another early 19th century *conac* belonging to the Konopi family at Konop village close by. Recently the village school, it is now empty save for the loft which is stacked with pieces of broken kachelofen porcelain stoves that were gleefully smashed and shattered seventy years ago by bravado Party members as symbols of wealth and decadence.

In Tomeşti, Paddy's host, Robert, the last descendant of the family, died after the war in Bucharest and his ashes were placed in the family tomb in the crypt below the little Roman-Catholic chapel, donated to the village by the Losch family. The chandelier hanging in the middle of the chapel is decorated with crystals made from the first glass produced in the valley. The factory continued after the war and during the Communist regime received considerable investment both in plant and new housing for its workforce which peaked at around 1,600. After 1989, there were no buyers for this loss-making state-owned business and it finally closed after nearly two hundred years of glass making. In the long valley, sealed on either side by vertical tree-lined cliffs, the workers' apartment blocks in Colonia Fabricii are mainly empty, their owners forced to find work elsewhere. The plant now advertises the production of parquet tiles. The Winkler house with its staircases of forest trophies is hard to identify but it is most probably in the lower village, away from the once smoking stacks.

Xenia's family lost Zam in 1948. For a time, the house served as the village hospital but, since 1976, it has been a mental health institution, Spitalul de Psihiatrie Zam. There are two hospitals in the grounds, one in the old Castelul Nopcsa where Xenia lived and the other a purpose-built five story block from the 1970s by the main road. Barred windows on the pale yellow kastély indicate it houses dangerous inmates which the janitor later confirmed. The 'tall, exotic' arboretum of 'Himalayan and Patagonian trees' continues to flourish albeit in a somewhat unkempt fashion; the lake has long been drained.

Gurasada has slowly lapsed into ruination. On his first visit, Tom Fort found the videki kastély in a dilapidated state in the so-called care of the Ministry of Agriculture. When he returned in 2008, the house looked beyond 'hope of repair or redemption'. The bamboo grove had almost engulfed the loggia where Paddy and Elemér had sat through the summer nights, smoking hand-rolled cigarettes and when, 'if we were late enough, nightingales filled in the rare gaps in our talk'. Three years later Nick Hunt passed by, noting that 'nothing stirred inside but dust'.

Paddy's description of Gurasada as 'a mixture of manor house, monastery and farmstead' is a touch exaggerated for there is little evidence here of a monastic cloister or church. The kastély is a modest, single storey house on an elevated base with cellars beneath. Incredibly, the green and purple panes that once 'glimmered in the fanlight at the far end of an arcade' have survived, set above the door leading to the loggia. Inside the 'long disintegrating drawing-rooms', the floors are littered with the plastic bottled debris of modern day trysts. Of the tennis court 'sunk among thick trees like a shady well', nothing remains. The 'stables, granaries and coachhouses with carriages, wagons and sleighs' housed on either side of the gatehouse struggle to stay upright under the weight of a collapsing roof. The colonnades that lined the other three sides of the yard have been uprooted and removed. The bamboo thrives and has erected a scraggy screen on the outside of the loggia that obscures the heavens: no chance today of seeing constellations or meteors shower down the night sky.

Today if you go to Băleni, you will find a countryside of wide valleys with poppy-lined roads skirting undulating giant fields of wheat, of gently sloping hills clad with oak and lime and poplar, of wild flowers and nervous nesting plovers and orange-crowned hoopoes in butterfly-like flight. The village has grown considerably since Paddy's day with shops and bars and a new school. Constantin's and the sisters' new church, dedicated to St Helena and St Constantine, continues to be the centre of worship. Behind the open three arch porch with its pastel shaded frescos lies a pristine interior, lovingly restored by the Galați diocese and maintained with attentive fuss by the village priest.

Of the *conac*, nothing remains, all traces of the Cantacuzino Princely Court having been systematically eradicated after the Communists appropriated it as the office for the co-operative farm and then burnt it down. The park where it once stood has been flattened and built over with houses and clusters of sheds and outhouses. Only the family crypt remains, hidden in the midst of the trees and unruly long steppe grasses of the old village graveyard. Here are the tombs of Gheorghe and his wife Fanny, Leon and Anna, Balașa and Pomme alongside three other family members – little Constantin Cantacuzino, Gheorghe's son who died aged 11 months in 1883; Aristia Ghika-Deleni, Balașa's great-grandmother; Gheorghe Farcas; and Constantin Donici. Ina, Pomme's daughter, is buried in Paris and with her the line ended.

The great library at Băleni, assembled by the family from 1829 onwards and admired by the historian Nicolae Iorga in 1927 for its 'artistic and rare editions', probably numbered 10,000 items in its heyday, with manuscripts and books in English, French, Russian, Greek, German and Romanian. Beginning on the night of 2/3 March 1947 when Balașa and her sister and brother-in-law were unceremoniously evicted, the precious collection slowly haemorrhaged; some volumes came to a charcoaled end burning in the bottom of a decommissioned root cellar, others were thrown into a nearby river or used to pave muddy paths[16]. One villager told of pyres of burning books that smoked for months on end.[17] Another story recounts how peasants fashioned shoes out of the luxurious Burgundy-coloured silk bindings. Fortunately, over 1,200 have found their way to the

---

[16] Some books were destroyed in 1944 when Balașa's Bucharest appartment was bombed by the Allies.

[17] Father Nechifor to author, June 2017.

'V.A. Urechia" library[18] in Galați where they are once more treasured and appreciated.

One architectural memento of Băleni did survive – a fireplace. Paddy had first met the famous Romanian architect Georges Cantacuzino in Bucharest, 'hotfoot from a long journey through Persia'. At Băleni, to a design by Georges, he helped build a 'Persian' fireplace in Pomme and Constantin's bedroom. It was the memory of this that inspired him to replicate it at Kardamyli. He wrote to Marie-Lyse Ruhemann, Georges's daughter, how he'd copied it 'out of your father's Persian sketch book certainly [?] now lost in Romania. If so, here it survives, at two removes, like part of all those traditions in architecture brought back from the Crusades and subsequently slightly altered'.

With its conical chimney breast and broad cheeks of the surround, Paddy's fireplace was identical in every respect save that of a double-edge top to the firebox. 'I suppose I thought it looked even more picturesquely Persian and it was a mistake; it is too high, and, when a north wind blows, it smokes a bit'. Nonetheless, on a cold winter's evening in the Mani, as he gazed at the fire, Paddy was surely transported back to Romania which 'one misses…tremendously – even someone who has much less claim for dor[19] from it as me. But it has played such a large role in one's life'[20].

---

[18] Str. Mihai Bravu 16, Galați 800208, Romania.

[19] A longing for.

[20] Letter PLF to Marie-Lyse Ruhemann [née Cantacuzino] 3 February 2007.

BIBLIOGRAPHY

Paddy's Romanian bibliography:

Mani, Travels on the Southern Peloponnese [1958]

Introduction to Matila Ghyka's The World Mine Oyster [1961]

The Danube, Holiday Magazine, August [1966]

Between the Woods and the Water [1986]

Rumania–Travels in a Land before Darkness Fell, Daily Telegraph Weekend Magazine, 12 May 1990

Introduction to Sacherverell Sitwell's Roumanian Journey [1992]

Introduction to Miklós Bánffy's Transylvania Trilogy [1999]

Words of Mercury [2003]

The Broken Road [2013]

Other books:

Botiş, Dr Teodor: Monografia Familiei Mocioni, King Carol II Foundation for literature and art, Bucharest [1939]

Callimachi, Princess Anne-Marie: Yesterday was Mine [1949]

Cantacuzène, Jean Michel: A Prince among Communists [2015]

Cooper, Artemis: Paddy Leigh Fermor, an Adventure [2013]

Debita, Gabriela: Fondul Cantacuzino at Bibliotecii V.A.Urechia Galați Vols 1 and 2

Fenwick, Simon: Joan [2017]

Fort, Tom: Against the Flow [2010]

Goldsworthy, Vesna: Inventing Ruritania [1998]

Ghyka, Matila: The World Mine Oyster [1961]

Hunt, Nick: Walking the Wood and the Water [2014]

Manning, Olivia: The Great Fortune [1960] and The Spoilt City [1962]

Paltanea, Paul: Note Genealogice Despre Cantacuzini de la Băleni, Editura Academiei Romane, Iasi [1996]

Pantazzi, Ethel: Roumania in Light and Shade [1921]

Patmore, Derek: Invitation to Romania [1939]

Patmore, Derek: Images of Greece [1944]

Patmore, Derek: Private History [1960]

Pintilie, Dorin and Mariana: Comuna Băleni, Studi Monographic Complex, Editura Eurodidact, Cluj [2003]

Seton Watson, Robert: A History of the Roumanians [1934]

Sitwell, Sacherverell: Roumanian Journey [1938]

Sturdza, Mihai Dim.: Familiile boieresti din Moldova si Tara Romaneasca. Enciclopedie istorica, genealogica si biografica, vol. III, Familia Cantacuzino [2016]

Waldeck, Rosie: Athene Palace

ACKNOWLEDGEMENTS

With thanks to the late Şerban Cantacuzino for his ever-guiding hand and font of family knowledge; Geoffrey Cardozo for translating Balaşa's poem; Michael de Styrcea for all matters Mocsonyi and for his generous hospitality in Bata; Father Nechifor, the Parish priest of Băleni, who showed me around his church and inducted me in the history of Băleni; Gabriela Debita and Valentina Onet of the V.A. Urechia Library for keeping the memory of Balaşa alive; Prof Dennis Deletant for his invaluable help about 20th century Romania; Cristian Ferecatu for organizing my visit and driving me around Moldavia; Marie-Lyse Ruhemann for sharing her letters from Paddy; Vasile from Zabola for his photograph as a boy; Steven Tötösy de Zepetnek who steered me expertly through Hungarian history and social etiquette; Tom Fort and Nick Hunt for their pathfinding; Tennessee Blackmore for his photography in the Mureş valley; Peter of Pensiune 'Black Face' in Zam; Ovidiu Roşu from Bata; Lidia Bada of Casa Bata; Mark Lawson for hosting me in Edinburgh; and the ever helpful and efficient archive team at the National Library of Scotland.

Vasile, a Transylvanian shepherd boy on the Zăbala Estate [1936]